the Healing Garden

the Healing Garden

Heather B. Moore

USA Today Bestselling Author

Copyright © 2024 by Heather B. Moore
Paperback edition
All rights reserved.

No part of this book may be reproduced in any form whatsoever without prior written permission of the publisher, except in the case of brief passages embodied in critical reviews and articles. This is a work of fiction. The characters, names, incidents, places, and dialogue are products of the author's imagination and are not to be construed as real.
Interior design by Cora Johnson
Edited by JL Editing Services and Lorie Humpherys
Cover design by Rachael Anderson
Cover image credit: Deposit Photos #113085024, Egnis Moore
Published by Mirror Press, LLC
ISBN: 978-1-952611-43-8

THE HEALING SERIES:
The Healing Summer
The Healing Garden

EVERLY FALLS SERIES:
Just Add Romance
Just Add Mischief
Just Add Friendship

PINE VALLEY SERIES:
Worth the Risk
Where I Belong
Say You Love Me
Waiting for You
Finding Us
Until We Kissed
Let's Begin Again
All For You

PROSPERITY RANCH SERIES:
One Summer Day
Steal My Heart
Not Over You
Seasoned with Love
Take a Chance

HISTORICAL TITLES:
The Paper Daughters of Chinatown
The Slow March of Light
In the Shadow of a Queen
Under the Java Moon
Lady Flyer
Until Vienna
Love is Come

HISTORICAL UNDER H.B. MOORE:
Esther the Queen
Ruth
Deborah: Prophetess of God
The Moses Chronicles
Mary and Martha
Hannah: Mother of a Prophet
Rebekah and Isaac

Spring 1981

Eighty-three year old Sam Davis has always wondered what happened to his high-school sweetheart. But instead of finding the means to track her down, he's stuck in an assisted living center, reliant on others around him. His grandson, Wyatt, questions Sam's memories, and it seems that he'll never find the answers he's been searching for.

Anita Gifford, single mom in her mid-30s, is reluctant to spend community service hours at the assisted living center in their town. But her fourteen-year-old daughter Carly has to work off her school suspension. So instead of a relaxing weekend after a long week of work, Anita takes Carly to the center where they meet Mr. Davis. An unexpected bond forms between the teenager and elderly man, one that might bring healing to both families, past and present.

One

Spring 1981

"Mrs. Gifford?"

"Yes?" Anita winced at the formal title because it could mean only one thing—the phone call was from the middle school.

"This is Debbie Nelson, calling from Monroe Middle School," the woman said in a stern tone.

The twisting in Anita's stomach told her it wasn't a good-news call. She walked with the receiver, its cord stretching, to look out the large front window at the small yard and cracked sidewalk beyond.

"I've called with regretful news." Debbie paused. "Your daughter Carly has misbehaved, and she's been given a suspension by our principal, Mr. Mortenson."

As if Anita didn't know the principal's name. They'd had more than one meeting . . . "What happened?" Her tone sounded sharp, but it was too late to change that now.

"Carly and a group of her friends decided to ditch second period and raid the kitchen."

"*Raid?*"

"What someone does when they steal food that doesn't belong to them," Debbie Nelson said.

Anita dragged in a breath and focused on using normal words that didn't involve any cussing. "Where is Carly now?"

"Waiting to be picked up by a parent," Debbie said. "She said it was only her mom since there's no Mr. Gifford in the picture?"

Anita tightened her hold on the receiver and wondered if it would be too childish to pick up one of the picture frames on the bookcase and throw it. Or maybe she should throw a book. Something. Anything.

Another steadying breath. "No, there's no Mr. Gifford in the picture, Ms. Nelson. I'll be there in ten minutes."

Anita hung up the phone and closed her eyes for a handful of seconds, trying to keep the scream of frustration inside. How had this become her life? Living in Seattle as a single mom? A year ago, she and Carly had been best friends, bosom buddies, doing everything together. Then Carly turned fourteen, started ninth grade, and poof. It was all gone. She had been swept into a new friend group and undergone a complete personality change.

"Meow." A furry head bumped against her ankles.

"Me too, Sassy," Anita mumbled, opening her eyes. The gray tabby meowed again, then trotted to the front door, waiting to be let outside.

She replaced the phone receiver, then grabbed her car keys off the top of the fridge. Her hands trembled, not because she was nervous or cold, but because her anger was making her shake.

Carly had been given everything in life—well, everything Anita could provide as a single mom. She'd been able to make a career out of her creative talents so that she wasn't an absent parent. She was at home every day after school. She was there every morning to fix school lunch and see her daughter off. Anita scrounged up fun things to do on the weekends, plus stayed flexible with what Carly wanted to do.

The Healing Garden

Mostly, they'd go on short road trips to check out a hiking trail, a park, a zoo, or a botanical garden. Sometimes they'd stay overnight, or drive late to get back home. Anita's favorite thing to do was to not have a particular destination or agenda. Just get into the car and drive, letting adventure come naturally. Although lately, Carly had wanted to stay home on weekend nights, talking on the phone, if she wasn't hanging out at a friend's house.

Anita had even budged on the curfew. Eight on school nights and ten on weekends.

All these thoughts spun through her mind as she opened the front door, and Sassy zoomed outside. Anita headed toward her Volkswagen Bug that had seen better days. She'd bought it with her first few art commissions when Carly was a baby, and the car had been treating them well. Except for this week. She'd had trouble starting it.

She eyed her sky-blue Bug as she approached. Would she be a good girl today?

"Hello-oo!" a woman's voice called. The singsong tone was unmistakable.

"Hi, Phyllis," Anita said to her neighbor, who stood by the mailbox between their properties. She was a seventy-something widow who seemed to always be around when Anita stepped outside her door.

"Want me to grab your mail?" Phyllis pushed up her gold-framed glasses. "If you're in a hurry, I can keep it at my house until you return."

Anita hid a grimace. Her nosy neighbor had just out-done herself. "Oh, it's fine. I have time to grab the mail."

"Oh, hello there, Sassy," Phyllis said as the cat rubbed against her calves. She bent to give the cat a scratch.

As Anita approached, her neighbor stopped petting the cat and snapped open Anita's mailbox and plucked out the handful of letters that were probably bills.

"Thank you." Anita held out her hand.

"You're heading out for some errands?" Phyllis seemed to reluctantly let go of the mail pieces.

"I'm going to a meeting at the school," Anita said, then immediately regretted giving her that much information. "A . . . a parent meeting."

Phyllis folded her arms, crinkling her own collection of letters. "Is everything all right? Aren't parent meetings usually in the morning?"

Anita had no idea what this woman was referring to. "This one isn't. Thanks for the mail. I'll see you later." She hurried away from Phyllis and toward her car.

Once she slid into the driver's seat of the Bug, she could only hope that it would start, since Phyllis was still hovering at the mailbox, watching.

"Please start," Anita muttered as she turned the key. The engine sputtered to life—not quite the purr that would say *all was well*, but at least it had started. She wasn't about to be picky, and she really didn't have extra money for a car repair right now. Not with yesterday's purchase of summer clothes for Carly.

She backed out of the driveway, jostled by the eroding concrete, then pulled onto the road. The school was only a mile away, but she was already sweating with the warming April weather and didn't want to delay picking up her daughter.

Her *suspended* daughter.

Anita gritted her teeth as she pulled into the school's parking lot. Were the other parents arriving now too? She hadn't even checked her appearance before leaving—it had been the last thing on her mind. But now that she was at the school parking lot, she knew there was a good chance of running into the moms. The women who mothered Carly's friends were all the same type of women. None of them worked outside the home, and they all seemed to have plenty of money, plus extra for hair-coloring jobs, manicured nails, and clothing that hadn't been purchased from the Salvation Army.

Anita wasn't embarrassed to shop at a thrift store, because she wanted to cut as many corners as she could, while spending any extra on Carly.

Just as she pulled in, a Saab convertible flew past her, then parked in the handicap spot. Oh, and the other moms had much nicer cars.

Vera Hessington climbed out of the convertible, tossed her long red hair, then practically waltzed toward the front doors of the school. Her step bounced, probably due to the fact that she wore tennis clothes, as if she'd just walked off the court. And she probably had. Anita imagined one of the busboys at the country club, where Vera spent her days, rushing over to inform her she had an important phone call.

"It's fine," Anita mumbled to herself. She might be thirty-five, single, and living commission check to commission check, but she was happy. Generally. When her little girl wasn't cutting classes and getting suspended. She released a breath and headed into the school after Vera disappeared inside. Was it terrible to just want her little girl back? To want to rewind time a few years to when they'd check out videos together, then rush home and argue about which one they'd be popping into the VCR first?

Anita tugged open the front door and a gust of musty swamp-cooler air rushed out. The entrance was empty and quiet, which meant she could hear Vera's rather shrill voice. Probably talking to the principal.

"I'll make sure she shadows someone in the country club kitchen this week, Mr. Mortenson," she said as Anita approached the front office. "You won't need to worry about

Samantha again. She'll be here bright and early on Monday, ready to work hard."

Anita stepped inside the office, but no one noticed her. A couple office ladies sat behind their desks, pretending not to be eavesdropping, and Principal Mortenson was nodding at Vera, a pleased look on his round-cheeked face. He pushed up his glasses and extended his hand to the other mother. "Thanks for your cooperation, ma'am. You have a great girl here, but we need to uphold the school rules. Be sure to send her back with a signed note."

He flashed a smile, and Vera flashed one back. Then she turned, her hand clamped on Samantha's elbow. Both mother and daughter wore amused expressions, as if they were in on some private joke.

Anita stepped aside to let them pass. Vera gave her a small nod, her pink-lipsticked mouth pursed—otherwise, there was no eye contact between the mothers.

"Mrs. Gifford," the principal said, turning to her. "Carly is this way."

As Anita followed him down the short hallway to his private office, she noted that no other kids were around, so maybe it had been just Samantha and Carly?

Anita slowed when she saw Carly—her tear-stained face, red-rimmed eyes, and her carefully curled hair hanging limply about her shoulders. Her hair had darkened over the past year. When she was a toddler, Anita used to call her a golden girl because her hair was a shade of gold. Now it was more of a medium brown.

"Hi, Mom," she said in a near-whisper, and Anita's heart completely melted.

Carly might have done something stupid, but she was only a kid. A kid who was trying to figure things out and navigate friendships.

"Hi," she said in a soft voice. "Are you okay?"

The Healing Garden

Carly's eyes welled with new tears, and she sniffled.

Principle Mortenson adjusted his glasses, then clasped his hands together. "Mrs. Gifford, you might have heard some of what we arranged with Mrs. Hessington. The girls are expected to put in eight community service hours before returning to school. I suggest getting them all done over the weekend, or Carly will be marked truant on Monday."

Clearly, her daughter had heard all of this, because she didn't react.

Community service hours, though? It wasn't like Anita could send Carly to the country club with a snap of her fingers. They'd have to make phone calls. She met the principal's gaze. "Does anything need to be done at the school? Carly could start here."

He shook his head. "Afraid not. You might check with the library or the senior center. There's also an assisted living home at the edge of town. Or the bowling alley." He shrugged. "They could use help cleaning that place."

Anita agreed, but weren't bowling alleys supposed to be grungy? "All right, thank you."

As they headed out of the office, the principal regaled Carly with another warning, and although Anita wanted her daughter to learn her lesson, she also felt irked. As soon as they were outside, she asked, "Was it just you and Samantha?"

"No," Carly said. "Evie too. She got picked up first. It's not fair, though."

"What's not fair? That Evie got picked up first? Or that you were caught raiding the kitchen?"

"No," Carly said as they neared the car.

When she hesitated, Anita said, "Out with it. You're going to be grounded anyway, so you might as well tell me everything."

Carly ducked her head and reached for the door handle. She had to tug hard to get the car door open.

Anita slid into the driver's side and set her hands on the wheel. "Explain please."

What came out was a disjointed story, with Carly saying it was a dare, and it was stupid, and she regretted it. She relied on the sincerity of her daughter's tone, which ended in a few more tears, and she decided that the girl felt guilty enough and didn't need to be berated more.

"All right, I understand doing something stupid—but please don't do anything like that again," Anita said. "You'll be grounded from those friends for two weeks, and you need to make the phone calls when we get home to figure out how to get those service hours in."

Carly gave a nod and wiped at her face.

Anita dug out a tissue packet from her purse and handed it over. While Carly dried her tears, she released the brake, then put the car into neutral and turned the key in the ignition. The engine turned over once, then died.

"Great," she muttered. "Of all places." She blew out a breath, then tried to start the car again. Nothing. "We need to jump it."

Carly groaned, but opened her door. She climbed out, then braced her hands, preparing to help push.

Anita climbed out as well. Together, they pushed clear of other cars, then jumped back in when they reached the slope that led to the main road. She popped the clutch, and the car started. "Yes!" she yelled, and both of them smacked the roof of the car.

It was for good luck—but how long would that luck last?

"I think we're going to be buying a new battery this weekend," Anita said. "I hope that's all it is."

Carly's tears were gone, and they weren't stuck in the school parking lot. Anita decided to be grateful for the small things.

Two

AN HOUR LATER, CARLY CAME into the backyard, where Anita had set up a utility table next to the herbal garden. Her latest creation was a commissioned piece from an older lady who'd wanted her late husband's likeness created out of plant material and leaves. He'd been an avid outdoorsman before his death, and the widow had mailed photos of him, along with his favorite flannel shirt.

"Is that from the dead guy?" Carly asked, recognizing the project.

"Be respectful," Anita said.

Carly puffed out a breath. "Well, he's dead, right? What else should I say?"

Was her daughter really going to start with the attitude an hour after her suspension? "His name was Roger Barton, so you can refer to him as *Mr. Barton.*" Anita set down the bit of rosemary she'd been using to create the effect of hair. She folded her arms. "Well?"

Carly shifted from one foot to the other. She'd combed her hair into a ponytail, and it looked like all the curl had fallen out. Like Anita, she had no natural curl, and it could only be achieved by wearing curlers all night or using their old curling iron that didn't get very hot anymore. Her daughter usually opted for the curlers.

"I called all of the places," Carly said, her tone sounding uncertain. "And . . ."

Anita waited, wanting her to take ownership in this process.

"And . . . the assisted living place said I could come and play games or read with the old people."

Anita winced. "*Old* people? You mean the residents?"

"Whatever."

She tried not to bristle. "All right. That's a good idea. When are you going?"

Carly's eyes widened. "Uh, tomorrow, I guess. But I don't want to go alone."

Anita sat back in her chair. "I can take you to the place, but this is *your* service, Carly, not mine. I have plenty to do here."

Carly looked down at the ground, her sandal scuffing the paving stones. "They said I needed your permission."

"I can send a note."

Carly looked up again. "I think they want it over the phone. The lady is waiting right now to talk to you."

Anita shot up from her chair. "You left her on the phone and waited to tell me?" She didn't pause for an answer, hurrying to the back door that led to the kitchen.

"Hello-oo, Anita! Oh, is that you, Carly?" Phyllis had come out into her backyard, which shared a fence with theirs.

How long had she been standing there and what had she heard?

"Hi, Phyllis," Anita said. "I need to answer the phone."

"Oh, you go right ahead." Phyllis held up rose clippers. "I'm just trimming a few roses. By the way, Sassy is over here, and I fed her some tuna."

"Oh, all right. Thank you." Anita stepped into her house. She found the receiver on the kitchen table. "Hello? This is Mrs. Gifford. Sorry to make you wait."

The Healing Garden

The woman's voice that came through the phone was completely nonplussed and cheerful. "No worries, Mrs. Gifford. This is Nancy. I've had a nice chat with your delightful daughter, and we're looking forward to seeing the two of you tomorrow."

Delightful daughter? "I think there's been a mistake," Anita said. "This is a service project for Carly. I'll drop her off, then pick her up when she's done."

The other end went silent for a moment, then Nancy said, "I think there's been a misunderstanding, perhaps? Since Carly is a minor, she needs to have a parent in the building while she's spending time with the residents."

Anita frowned and turned to gaze out the window overlooking the garden. Carly was crouched near the late tulips, inspecting something. "Well, I wasn't aware of that." She dragged in a breath. "I have a busy schedule just now, and I'm happy to sign a permission form. You see—"

"We can't accept that," Nancy said, her voice still kind. "I understand busy. I raised three kids myself—on my own. I've been in your shoes as a single mom."

Anita's mouth parted. What had Carly told this stranger over the phone?

"But sometimes, you have to make the sacrifice of *time*," Nancy said. "Carly told us she needs eight hours, and so we are accommodating your family, not the other way around."

Well. The woman was certainly direct. And right. "I'm sorry," Anita said. "I didn't mean to . . . I guess what I'm trying to say is . . ." Her thoughts were so jumbled that she had no idea what she was trying to say.

"Look, Mrs. Gifford," Nancy continued in her gentle, calming voice, "Carly's a good kid. You showing up for her will only strengthen that relationship as she's adjusting to adolescence. We all make mistakes."

"Did Carly tell you that . . ."

When her voice dropped off, Nancy said, "She explained everything. And if you can agree to our terms, we'll see you tomorrow afternoon from two to six p.m., and then again on Sunday. Same time."

Anita had no idea if her daughter had called the other places, or if they also required that a parent be on the premises. "All right. That's fine. We'll be there tomorrow at two o'clock."

Nancy cheerfully gave her directions, which Anita decided not to interrupt, though she already knew where the assisted living facility was. After hanging up, she found Carly in the garden. She was still crouched next to the tulips, and on her hand crawled a ladybug.

The sight brought back a flood of memories of Carly as a little girl, following her around the garden, asking nonstop questions, helping do small tasks, and her endless fascination with the bugs. Anita's irritation abated.

"I talked to Nancy."

Carly looked up.

"Next time you have someone waiting to speak with me, tell me that first."

Carly nodded. "Okay."

"I guess I have to go with you," Anita said in the most even tone she could muster. "Go get your homework done, and I'll let you know when dinner is ready. You're on cleanup duty, and tomorrow morning, you'll have some other chores before we go to the facility."

Carly nodded again, her expression sheepish. Then she headed past Anita, who noticed she had the ladybug latched on to her wrist.

Anita hid a smile, then stood for a quiet moment in the garden. As much as she wanted to return to her project, she should probably preempt her car's maintenance troubles. She guessed that most auto shops closed at five or six p.m., which meant she had to start calling now to track down a battery.

After a handful of phone calls, she had the battery priced out. Everyone would be closed on the weekend, so it needed to be her top priority on Monday. Surely her car could behave until then, even if it required another jump-start.

Meanwhile, she pulled out a box of Hamburger Helper. Not her favorite meal, but a childhood favorite of Carly's. There was hamburger meat in the freezer, so she took it out and set it in a pan of warm water to begin thawing. She should have started this all earlier, but Carly's original plans had been to hang out at Samantha's house tonight, and have dinner there. Anita had planned on having a sandwich solo.

Just as she was pulling out a few salad fixings from the refrigerator, the phone rang. She answered, and it was Samantha on the other line.

"Carly, it's Samantha," Anita called out.

In record time, she appeared from her bedroom.

"Keep it short," Anita said before Carly picked up the receiver.

"Hi," Carly said, then headed down the hallway, the long cord trailing after her. "I can't. I'm grounded."

That was the last Anita heard of the conversation before Carly disappeared into the bedroom. She wondered if Samantha was grounded. And what about Evie? Was grounding the right thing to do with a fourteen-year-old? Would something else be more effective? She didn't want to push Carly too far, but she also didn't want her daughter suspended from school.

She began to rip up the iceberg lettuce. She'd make a Caesar salad because Carly was sure to eat that. When Anita had been in school, she'd never considered stealing or vandalizing. But then again, her single best friend hadn't been the type to do that either. So maybe she had just been lucky with her friend choice. Not that she had a ton of choices. She seemed to say awkward things in social situations, so she hadn't been the type of teenager to have a gaggle of friends or get invited to the cool-kid parties. She'd kept to herself most of the time, unless she was with her best friend.

The conversation between Carly and Samantha was officially past "keep it short," but something tugged in Anita's heart, and she couldn't bring herself to give Carly a warning. She set the bowl of lettuce aside and checked on the thawing meat. It was mostly soft, so she set the frying pan on the stove and turned on the element. The meat began to sizzle right away, and she filled a pot with water to begin boiling the pasta from the Hamburger Helper box.

A few minutes later, Carly came out of her bedroom, her expression sullen.

Anita couldn't help but ask, "Are your friends grounded too?"

"No," she said. "Their moms are letting them hang out tonight." She turned her sad eyes on her mother. "They want me to come over."

Anita wished she could say yes—she *wanted* to say yes—but wasn't getting suspended from school kind of serious? And why were the other parents not being more strict? "No, I can't go back on our agreement."

Carly huffed and walked back to her room.

What were the chances she was actually doing homework? Again, an ache pinched Anita's heart as she wished she had her little girl back. She stirred in the pasta, added a dash of salt, then used the spatula to dice up the hamburger into smaller pieces.

The Healing Garden

The phone rang again, and she wiped off her hands to answer it.

"Anita?" the deep voice said. "How are you?"

Her arms broke out in goose bumps, and she didn't know if it was in a good way. "Hi, Glenn."

"What are you doing?"

The question irritated her because after their last date, he said he'd call her the next day and figure out something to do the next weekend. He'd never called. And now it was the following weekend, but Anita wasn't going anywhere with Carly stuck at home. Carly would probably love her to leave, so that was out of the question.

Anita had attempted dating this past year. Previously, she hadn't wanted anything to interfere with raising Carly, even though she knew that having a father figure in her daughter's life would be of value. With Carly's social life picking up on the weekends, it gave Anita a little more freedom than she was used to.

"Making dinner," she told Glenn. "What are you doing?"

"Hmm." His voice was a low rumble, which might have been sexy, but it was only irritating right now. "What's for dinner?"

"Hamburger Helper."

Glenn laughed. "I haven't had that in forever. Which box? Maybe I'll come over."

"Uh..." Anita was already tired of the twenty-questions game. "Doesn't really matter because I don't want any company tonight. It's just me and Carly." For some reason, she didn't want to tell him about Carly's suspension.

"Girls only, huh?" Glenn asked, then lowered his voice. "What about *after* hours? Carly goes to bed around ten, right?"

They'd been on three official dates, and a couple of meetups at city events. Anita sensed that Glenn liked her more than she liked him, but that he wasn't exactly fully invested. He sort of disappeared for a while, then suddenly reappeared. They'd almost kissed on the last date, but then it hadn't happened. Anita had been disappointed at the time, but right now she was feeling kind of glad. Strange.

Was her heart still that messed up from Carly's dad?

"Let's talk next week sometime." Anita felt more than a little hungry. She didn't want to deal with Glenn right now, which was another strange thing. When she'd met him, she'd been charmed and was excited he'd asked her out on a date. Life had been much simpler then—and the past few hours had changed all of that.

"Sure thing," Glenn said in an easy tone, as if he were already thinking of someone else. "We'll talk next week."

Three

"Hi, Gramps, how are you doing?"

Sam Davis already knew what was coming. His grandson only called on the days he was canceling. He adjusted the receiver against his ear—lately he'd had trouble hearing as clearly as he liked. "Doing about the same as yesterday."

"Oh, that's great to hear," Wyatt said in a rush. "Really great. Hey, uh, look, I've had some things come up, and I'm afraid I won't make it this afternoon. But I can stop by tomorrow, if that's all right?"

"I'm not going anywhere," Sam said. And he wasn't. He'd been banished to this assisted living place a few months ago, and so far, he hated it. *You'll meet new friends,* they'd said. *You'll love having all your meals prepared for you,* they'd said. *There are so many activities,* they'd said. *You'll enjoy reminiscing with the others,* they'd said.

It was all hogwash, and he didn't really need to be here. So what if he'd fallen a couple of times. He'd been able to get up—eventually—and he refused to use a wheelchair. No matter how long it took him to make his way to the dining room or the other activities, a walker was better than a wheelchair. His body was turning against him, choosing the good days and bad days without his input. This morning had been good, but with the news of Wyatt's cancellation, Sam might as well just stay in his room for the rest of the day. Do some reading, which would probably turn into napping. So be it.

He reached for the book on the coffee table in front of him and turned to his bookmark. He adjusted his glasses and read a half page of the large-type print, then realized he couldn't remember what was going on in the story, so he restarted the chapter. How far he got, he didn't know, because the next thing he knew, he was being awakened from a nice nap.

"Mr. Davis?" a young female voice said from his partially open doorway. "It's time for our activity. Do you want me to help you into the wheelchair?"

Sam blinked at the dark-haired woman, trying to clear his mind from the dream he'd been having about Susan . . . again. This time, she hadn't moved with her family. She'd decided to stay in Seattle and attend the community college. She'd been worried about a place to stay since room and board at the college was expensive. Sam had just been about to suggest they talk to his parents' neighbors when he'd been awakened.

"I'm skipping the activity," he said in a rasp. He cleared his throat. "My grandson's not coming today."

The woman named Ginny tilted her head, and her brown eyes went soft. "Oh, sorry to hear that. But I'm happy to take you anyway. You'll enjoy yourself, and I'd hate for you to stay cooped up in your room."

The whole place was like living in a coop.

Before Sam could protest, Ginny pulled the wheelchair out of the corner and grasped his arm. The woman was strong, he'd give her that—or maybe he'd weakened. Both were likely true.

"There you are," she said after she'd strong-armed him into the chair. "Now, would you like a lap quilt?"

The Healing Garden

"No, I don't want a lap quilt." What was he? An old man? He tried to keep the bite out of his tone, but he doubted he'd been successful.

Ginny, to her credit, didn't flinch or become upset. "We have lemon bars for dessert tonight. Do you like lemon bars?"

"I don't like getting powdered sugar all over me."

She laughed as she rotated the wheelchair toward the door. "I'll keep that in mind, Mr. Davis." She began to push, then stopped rather abruptly. "Oh, were you in the Air Force?"

She must have spotted the row of framed photos that Wyatt and Paula had insisted on setting up.

"It was called the Army Air Corps back then," he said.

Ginny reached for a photo and picked up the frame. He was standing in front of the B-29 Superfortress with his co-pilot Jeffrey. The man hadn't made it through the war.

"Is this World War II?" she asked, awe in her voice.

"Yes."

"Oh boy, did you fly in Europe?"

"I did."

Ginny angled the picture as if to get a better spot of light on it. "What was that like?"

"What was it like dropping bombs on cities?" Sam asked. "Hell."

She set the picture down carefully. "I'm sorry, Mr. Davis, I didn't mean to bring up bad memories."

He was already feeling guilty about his sharp retort. It had been honest, yes, but Ginny didn't need to be the target of his bad mood. He drew in a breath and decided he'd explain, but then she wheeled him right out of the room. The hallway was filled with a few other wheelchair-bound residents, also on their way to the activity. Whatever that would be.

Ginny was a brisk walker, and they overtook a couple of the residents. They reached the dining room, which apparently had been converted into a game room. Each table had two to three game boxes in the middle like a decorative centerpiece. Visitors were scattered among the residents.

"Here you are," Ginny said cheerfully. "These visitors don't have family here, and they're happy to spend time with you."

Before Sam could tell her to take him back to his room, she'd wheeled him to a table with a woman and a teenager—likely her daughter, if their similar looks of honey-brown hair and blue eyes were any indication. The woman gave him a faint smile, but the teenager's eyes had shuttered. She looked about as happy to be here as he was.

"Hello, sir, what's your name?" the woman asked.

"This is Sam Davis," Ginny interjected, setting the brakes on his wheelchair. She stood next to him. "This is Anita Gifford and her daughter, Carly. They're here all afternoon. Now, does anyone want some punch?"

"Sure, that would be great," Anita said. "What about you, Carly?"

Carly looked down at her hands, folded atop the table. "Okay."

As Ginny bustled away, Sam got right to the point. "I don't need company, if that's what you're here for. My grandson, who's an accountant, is too busy to visit. I was taking a perfectly good nap in my room before Ginny woke me up. So if you'd rather do something else with your Saturday, don't give me a second thought."

Carly lifted her chin and eyed him.

Sam unlocked the wheelchair brakes, then pushed back from the table. Maybe he'd get one of the other aides to wheel him back since Ginny wouldn't take no for an answer.

He'd just managed to rotate his wheelchair when the girl said, "Mr. Davis, we'd like to play at least one game with you. If that's all right?"

Surely, she'd been prompted by her mother. Sam might be a grump, but he wasn't rude. He looked over at the teenager. Her hands were clasped together so tightly that her knuckles had gone white.

"Are you on a mother-daughter outing? Maybe passing off something for the Girl Scouts?"

Carly's cheeks pinked. "Not really. I . . ." She gave a side glance toward her mother. "I was suspended from school yesterday, and I have to put in service hours before I can go back."

Well, this was interesting. "You were *suspended*? Did you change your grades or something?"

The girl had the decency to look mortified. Another glance at her mother, then, "No, my friends and I were dumb and raided the kitchen."

Sam didn't even hesitate. "What did you take? Something good?"

Carly's mouth quirked. "Not really. We grabbed a bag of carrot sticks and another one of green apples."

Sam didn't mean to laugh—it just came out. And it was his full belly laugh. The one that hadn't made an appearance in quite some time. The other residents looked over, of course, and Ginny arrived at the table just then with a tray of punch.

"Mr. Davis, are you all right?"

Sam drew in a breath, nodded, wheezed, then laughed again.

Across the table, Carly's mouth opened in surprise, as if she wasn't sure if she was allowed to laugh or not. And her mother . . . her expression could put a thundercloud to shame.

Sam grasped one of the cups and downed the punch as if he'd been crossing a desert until this very moment. "I'm sorry, ma'am," he said to the girl's mother. He used the edge of his sleeve to dab at his eyes. "Getting suspended is no lighthearted matter, but at least when you raid the kitchen, go for the dessert."

Ginny looked confused, as she should, but Anita Gifford's expression cleared. And Carly's lips twitched.

Sam raised a hand. "Not that I'm encouraging you to go back anytime soon, young lady. The best way to get through school and life in general is to follow most rules."

"*Most* rules?" Carly said, her voice less timid.

Ah, she'd caught that. Smart girl. "Some rules are absolutely necessary," Sam qualified. "But sometimes a rule has to be broken to save a life."

Both mother's and daughter's eyes widened.

Laughing had put Sam too much at ease around these ladies. "Now," he said, sliding over one of the game boxes. "What are we playing? Scrabble or Life?"

"Scrabble," Carly said immediately.

This surprised him. "Good choice." He pushed the game box toward her. "Get us set up, and your mother can keep score. My eyes aren't what they used to be."

Carly eagerly opened the box and set up the game.

"Tell us about yourself, Mr. Davis," Anita said in a polite tone. "Are you from Seattle originally?"

"I was born and raised here," Sam said. "Joined the Air Service out of high school to put myself through college."

Carly actually looked interested. He was impressed. He gave them the shortened version of his life. "Married, had a daughter, served a tour in the war, ran a furniture business after I retired from the Air Force, then I sold my business, and here I am in my golden years."

The Healing Garden

"How old are you?" Carly asked, her eyes wide again.

"Carly, that's not polite to ask," her mother cut in.

Sam lifted a hand. "I just turned eighty-three. Seems I have a balance problem, and my eyes are losing some vision. Can't be trusted on my own."

"Oh, that's terrible," Carly said.

It was probably the most accurate and sincere thing that had been said to him in a long time. "It is terrible. I have to read books with large print."

Carly wrinkled her nose.

"And they make me use a wheelchair in here," he complained. "Makes me feel like I'm eighty-four."

Carly laughed.

Sam chuckled.

Anita smiled.

Maybe game night with some strangers wasn't so bad.

Over the next couple of hours, they took turns beating each other in Scrabble. Carly came up with a few clever words too. "You must be a proud mom," Sam told Anita at one point. "You've got a smart daughter who's easy to talk to."

Anita's brows lifted, and Sam didn't miss the pleased look in her eyes.

"I assume she takes after you, unless there's a spelling-whiz Mr. Gifford?" he asked.

"My dad's a bad speller," Carly said. "I once got a birthday card from him, and he spelled 'sincerely' wrong. Turns out it was the last time I heard from him."

Sam blinked. "What?" Then his mind clicked. "Oh, are your parents..."

Carly filled it in for him. "They're divorced." She shrugged as if it were the most natural thing to tell a near-stranger. "Dad has another family now."

Sam was almost afraid to look at Anita—was this line of conversation upsetting her? He took a peek, and her expression was completely neutral. She caught him looking at her, though.

"Carly's dad and I were high school sweethearts," she said, "and I honestly don't remember if he was a good speller. He got okay grades." She looked at her daughter and said in a quieter tone, "I hadn't noticed the misspelling on that birthday card."

"You're a smart girl to notice those kinds of details," Sam continued. "I think it's safe to say your talent comes from your mother."

Both mother and daughter shared a smile, then Anita did an extraordinary thing. She looked at Sam and mouthed, "Thank you."

Four

THREE PHONE CALLS ON SUNDAY morning had put Anita in an excellent mood. They were all art commissions, and she'd be set financially for the next couple months. Besides, Carly had done her assigned chores without complaint, and now it was time to head to the assisted living center. Now, if only the car would behave.

"Do you think we'll be assigned to Mr. Davis again?" Carly asked as they climbed into the Bug. She'd also baked some cookies because one of the conversations she and the older man had gotten into was how much he missed home cooking.

Since Carly had made a double batch, Anita had told her to take a plate over to Phyllis. That had led to a longer conversation between the two, so now they were running a little late. *It's fine,* she told herself. Surely they wouldn't get turned away if they showed up late for the activity night.

"I don't know how it all works at the center," she said. "I think he was at our table because his family hadn't come. Maybe today they'll be there."

"Well, if they don't come, let's request him."

Anita smiled. "All right." She was pleased at Carly's interest in befriending the older man. He'd given plenty of life advice without making anything sound like a lesson. She turned the key in the ignition and the Bug jumped to life. Both she and Carly kissed their fingers and touched the roof.

"How was Phyllis?" Anita asked. "She seemed chatty."

"She's always chatty, Mom."

Anita smiled at that. "I suppose she is."

"She's just lonely, you know."

Anita glanced over at Carly as guilt pricked. "That's probably true. I haven't seen her son show up for a few weeks."

As they turned the next corner, Carly said, "Hey, Mom, do you think we can go to the video store tonight after my service hours are done?"

Anita didn't hesitate. "Sure. What kind of movie do you want to watch?"

"Something funny." Carly leaned forward in her seat. "I wonder if we could get Mr. Davis to tell us more about the Air Force. I think it's cool that he was a pilot during the war."

"Some people don't like to talk about their war experiences," Anita warned. "So you can't push him."

"I know." Carly let the subject drop.

Once they reached the center, she parked, and they headed inside. The day before, they'd been told that today was craft day. The residents were already filling the tables by the time they walked into the dining room.

"There he is," Carly said, pointing to where Mr. Davis sat alone at a table.

This morning, he wore a navy shirt, and he wasn't in a wheelchair. Maybe it had been a good walking day?

Before Anita could tell her to not bother the man, she hurried over to his table.

"Is your family coming today?" Carly asked.

"Not until later," he said, a smile appearing on his face. "Have a seat unless you have other plans."

The man's hair was mostly gray, but his eyebrows were

dark, telling Anita that he'd had dark hair when he was younger. His face was angular, which made him look stern when he wasn't smiling. But they'd quickly learned he had a soft side.

"We don't have other plans." Carly sat right next to him. "What's the craft?"

Mr. Davis scowled. "I don't know, but I hope it's not anything with yarn. That blasted stuff makes my fingers feel like noodles."

Carly laughed. "My mom uses yarn in her art. It's not too bad."

"Oh, is that right?" Mr. Davis glanced at Anita as she took her seat. "What kind of art?"

She had answered this question dozens of times. "I create portraits out of natural materials like leaves and flower petals."

His brows tugged together. "Is yarn natural?"

"Not quite," she said. "Sometimes I'll use fabrics or yarns in colors that represent the person."

He leaned back in his chair and threaded his hands together. "Interesting."

"She's making a portrait of a dead guy right now," Carly blurted out. "The man's wife sent a picture and a flannel shirt."

One side of Mr. Davis's mouth lifted. "I'd like to see one of your creations."

Anita smiled, wondering if that was possible since today was their last day.

"Please, Mom?" Carly asked. "We could come back next weekend."

Anita stared at her in surprise. "You want to come back next weekend?"

"I have to beat Mr. Davis at Scrabble," she said, as if it wasn't any big deal.

"Well, okay, we'll bring one of my projects that I'm working on."

Mr. Davis and Carly grinned at each other.

Anita's heart tugged. What was happening here? Carly was becoming . . . her old self. And it was due to Mr. Davis.

"Here you are," an aide said—the same one from the day before. Ginny. "These are faux stained-glass projects. You paint each piece, then glue them together. Putting them in a window or by a light source will bring out all the pretty colors."

"That sounds fun." Carly jumped in before Mr. Davis could say something negative.

It was written all over his face, and Anita held back a laugh. Maybe these two were good for each other. Maybe she didn't need to date a guy like Glenn and wonder if he'd be a decent father figure to her daughter. Maybe Carly would benefit more from being around a grandfather stand-in.

Her own parents were long gone, and Bobby's parents had never been in the picture much. They thought she was the temptress and the seducer of their precious son. There hadn't been any bonding between them and Carly as a baby, and once Bobby took off, that door had completely closed.

The next hour was actually fun. Carly and Mr. Davis both laughed at their conversation, which bounced from painting their project and stories of selling furniture to "tight wads" and crushes both of them had in elementary school. Anita had heard about Carly's, of course—back when she told her mother everything—but Mr. Davis's story was interesting.

"It was always Susan from the moment I saw her," he said, dragging a brush with a careful hand over the plastic shape on the table before him. "I was fascinated by her bright red hair. Much like Pippy Longstocking's. Ever read those books?"

Carly's eyes brightened. "I did—my mom read them to me when I was little. Until I learned to read them myself."

"Then you know what I'm talking about," Mr. Davis said with a wink. "We both planned to attend the same college, then get married. But the world had other plans."

Carly's brow furrowed.

"The war?" Anita asked. Obviously Mr. Davis had survived it, but what about Susan?

"The economy struggled," he said, dipping his paintbrush again. "It wasn't the Depression yet, but after World War I, a lot of people were out of jobs. Her dad lost his job, and her family moved during our junior year of high school. Her father had found a job with her uncle's company in Carson, Nevada."

Anita was surprised by the pain still in Mr. Davis's voice. Had he never seen her again? Had his childhood crush been that strong?

"Did you write letters to each other?" Carly asked.

"We sure did," he said. "We called a few times too, but they were very short phone calls. Long distance was very expensive."

"But surely when you both graduated, you had more freedom?" Anita asked, becoming invested in the story.

"We made plans, but they fell through." Mr. Davis set his paintbrush down and met Anita's gaze, then looked over at Carly. "We were going to see each other over Christmas break. I was in my first year of college, and she was training to be a hairstylist. That was December 1920. But her mother died of the Spanish flu, which ran rampant through Nevada."

He dipped his paintbrush into the green paint. "I couldn't expect her to come to Seattle, and not many were traveling for fun or taking vacations. Too many deaths going on."

He painted a few strokes, then paused. Both Anita and Carly were staring at him, waiting for him to continue.

"By the time the scare was over, Susan had found another fellow." His hand trembled slightly as he continued to paint. "I met Norma a few months later, and we raised a daughter together. Norma was a wonderful woman, and we had a good life. She died a few years ago, and I miss her every day."

Anita didn't know why her eyes were burning with tears. Maybe it was the way that Mr. Davis obviously missed his wife, or maybe it was the forlorn way he looked when he spoke about his first love.

"Did you ever see Susan again?" Carly asked.

Anita winced, wondering if the question was too personal.

"I didn't," Mr. Davis said, his tone brighter now. "She stopped writing letters, of course, and we both moved on. I don't even know how many children or grandchildren she has now. Although..."

"Although what?" Carly pressed.

Mr. Davis breathed out slowly. "About a year ago, I received a postcard with no return address on it. It was a Medford postmark, though. There was a very short message, and it was signed by Susan."

Carly gasped, and Anita could only stare.

"What did the message say?" Carly asked.

Apparently Mr. Davis wasn't holding anything back from his new confidante. "She wrote, 'I hope life is swell. Sincerely, Susan.' No last name, but it could only be her."

"Did she spell 'sincerely' right?"

Mr. Davis chuckled. "She did."

"Are you talking about that postcard again, Gramps?" a man said, approaching their table.

The Healing Garden

Anita could only assume he was Mr. Davis's grandson—a man in his mid-thirties, with dark blond hair and green eyes. Wyatt didn't look like an accountant, unless a Clark Kent-type was an accountant.

His looks and height made her wonder if his grandmother or mother had been blonde with green eyes? Had their daughter been too? Wyatt was tall, over six feet, and Anita guessed Mr. Davis to be around five ten. Not that a grandson couldn't be several inches taller than a grandfather, but it just made her all the more curious.

She assured herself that her curiosity had nothing to do with the fact that Wyatt was a good-looking man, who wasn't wearing a wedding ring. She pushed that thought away because it was a thought that should have never entered her mind, and she was just here with her daughter to get service hours in.

"Wyatt, you made it." Mr. Davis extended his hand.

Wyatt grasped it, but also leaned close to hug the man. "I told you I was coming."

"You did." Mr. Davis patted his grandson on the back. "But I know you've been busy lately with tax season."

"If I can't take Sundays off to visit my grandpa, what's the meaning of life?" Wyatt shed the suitcoat he wore over a button-down shirt, then took a seat on the other side of his grandfather.

Mr. Davis grinned. "You didn't take the day off, did you?"

"I'm taking the afternoon off," Wyatt said.

"My grandson's an accountant, you know," Mr. Davis said. "Which means April is his busiest month with corporate taxes, and that's like a demanding wife."

Wyatt raised his hands. "Whoa, Gramps. Talk nice about my wife."

The interchange between grandfather and grandson was definitely interesting, Anita decided.

"Do you save companies from bankruptcy?" Carly asked.

Wyatt's green eyes cut to her. "Not exactly. That's for their lawyers to handle. I just run the numbers and file their taxes, for better or for worse. Who are you? New friends?"

"This is Carly and her mom, Anita," Mr. Davis said. "Carly is an expert Scrabble player and an artist like her mother."

Wyatt's brows lifted and his gaze focused solely on Anita. She didn't know why she felt scrutinized. Maybe it was the accountant in him?

"You're an artist?"

"I am." It was a simple question, but it also felt like a loaded one.

Wyatt surveyed the table, then looked at her again. "Are you running today's craft event?" He picked up one of the paintbrushes.

"No, I create portraits for individual clients."

Wyatt nodded, but a line had appeared between his brows.

"She uses stuff from our garden," Carly said. "Stuff I help plant."

Wyatt met her gaze. "So it's a collaborative effort?"

Carly's cheeks pinked. "More like chores."

Mr. Davis chuckled, and Wyatt smiled.

Anita hadn't expected his smile. Well, it wasn't out of line, but she hadn't expected his smile to make his eyes lighter and make her pulse jump. She decided to attribute it to the fact that Glenn was currently annoying her, and she hadn't let her gaze stray for a long time.

Wyatt looked at Carly again. "Someday you'll be

The Healing Garden

grateful for your chores, because there's nothing worse than having a college roommate who doesn't know how to do the dishes and never throws away rotten food."

Carly's brows popped up. "Did that happen to you?"

"Sure did," he said. "But if you can already garden and grow things that turn into beautiful art made by your mother, then I'll bet you're more independent than most grownups. You could probably go to college right now."

Carly smirked, but Anita could see she was pleased at the compliment.

Wyatt's gaze shifted to Anita again. He didn't say anything, but didn't seem to have any qualms about just looking at her. She scrambled for something to say. "Where did you, ah, go to college?"

"San Diego," Wyatt said. "Far away enough to get out from under my grandpa's thumb, yet close enough to come home for holidays."

"Oh, he's exaggerating," Mr. Davis said with a wave of his hand. "Once he went to college, he became a complete stranger."

"What are you talking about?" Wyatt said, his gaze snapping to his grandpa. "I came back almost every month for one thing or another."

Mr. Davis tapped his chin. "Well, maybe you did. It was a long time ago." He smiled at Carly. "You want to put away all this painting stuff? We can get out Scrabble, and if you can beat my grandson, then I'll know you're a real expert."

Carly didn't waste a second. She popped up from the table and cleared everything off, leaving the painted faux glass on one edge. When she took the paintbrushes to wash in the sink, Mr. Davis said, "I'll help you."

Anita watched with surprise as he used his walker to go with Carly to the utility sink outside the dining room.

"You know, my grandpa told me about you and your daughter on the phone this morning," Wyatt said.

"Oh, so you know why we came in the first place."

He nodded. "Yeah, and I think it's great that you're spending time with people at this center, but you must know that my grandpa has been living inside his own memories for the past while. It's why he's here. For the physical as well as memory care."

"Does he have dementia?" she asked.

"Not diagnosed," Wyatt said. "At least not yet. Ever since he received that postcard, he's been telling some rather strange stories of his past—things I'd never heard of before. I can only conclude that they're made up."

Anita was surprised at this. Did he mean everything about Susan was made up? "Was the postcard real?"

"He showed it to me, but his name wasn't on it. Not even on the address. Susan could have been writing to anyone."

"Oh," Anita said. "That's interesting."

"Yeah, to say the least," Wyatt said. "I'm just glad the postcard didn't arrive when my grandma was alive. I'm sure hearing a fictional story about her husband's first love wouldn't have been easy to bear."

Anita nodded. What else could she do?

"So I need a favor from you," Wyatt said, lowering his voice. Carly and Mr. Davis were on their way back. "If he brings it up again, change the subject. I don't want his imagination to run away with him, or pretty soon he'll be convinced that it was all real."

Anita didn't say that Mr. Davis had already convinced her it was real. "Okay," she said, but something felt off, because the look in Wyatt's eyes told her he wasn't entirely convinced Susan was a fictional.

Five

1919

SAM WAS READY TO TELL her. But how do you tell your best friend that you've been in love with her for years? Would Susan think he was a fraud? They'd shared their deepest thoughts. They'd spent weekends together going to the library to study, going to the cinema, or bowling with their group of friends. When they were kids, they rode bikes, built a treehouse, and collected bugs for an insect collection.

He couldn't think of a time when Susan wasn't the first person he wanted to talk to. Anything that happened in his life, he wanted to tell her.

And now, he needed to tell her this.

In the school halls that afternoon, he'd overheard a group of guys talking about who they were going to invite to the spring dance. Susan's name had come up. Jerry wanted to ask her.

Sam knew for a fact that Susan didn't have a crush on Jerry, but she thought he was a swell enough guy. That might change if they went on a fancy date, and she might start to like him. Sam had been privy to all of Susan's crushes over the years. They started out strong, but fizzled quickly. They always laughed about that. Ironically, Sam never had crushes on other girls. Sure, he'd date, mostly double dating with

Susan and her current crush. But he had never wanted anyone more than he wanted her.

He found her in her backyard after knocking on her front door.

"Hey," he said, spying her lounging on the hammock with a book in her hand. She was always reading something, and invariably, he'd end up reading it, too, just so they could have a conversation about the book.

"Hey." Susan turned her head and gave him a lazy smile.

He loved her smile. He loved the way her lips quirked, and he loved the light blue of her eyes, and the freckles that seemed to dance along her skin.

"Your mom said you were back here. Are you busy?"

She held up the book. "Not really. Have you read *My Antonia*?"

"Not yet—you getting ahead in English class?"

"I've read it before," Susan said, moving to sit up on the hammock. She patted the space next to her.

Sam didn't hesitate to join her. Sitting next to her on the hammock would mean that their shoulders would be pressed together. He didn't mind, but he also wondered if it was the best situation to confess to her. "Of course you've read it before. Is it good?"

Susan laughed.

He loved her laugh too.

"Do you think our English teacher would assign a bad book?" She nudged his shoulder.

He nudged her back. "I guess not." She smelled of strawberries—he already knew it was her shampoo because she'd told him once.

She used her foot to propel them into a swaying motion. "Did you get the job?"

"No," Sam said. "They gave it to a man with a family. He's a war veteran."

Susan's brows lifted. "The gas station doesn't pay enough to support a family."

"It doesn't, but my folks say things are getting more desperate around here." He shook his head. With all the soldiers having returned from war, the jobs were snatched up in minutes.

"Yeah, my mom said we have to start scrimping more. No extras."

They swayed for a couple more minutes, then Sam said, "You thinking about going to the Spring Fling?"

Susan scrunched her nose. "That's weeks away. No one's asking yet."

"I overheard some guys talking about it."

She turned to look at him. "Already?"

"Yeah."

She lifted a shoulder. "I won't have a dress, so I'll probably stay home. Are you asking someone?"

"I want to ask someone, but I don't know if she'll say yes."

Susan gave a small laugh. "She'll say yes. You're a catch, Sam Davis."

"I am?"

"I mean, you shower, you're on the baseball team, you have goals in life, and you're not terrible looking."

He knew she was teasing, but what if she was serious too? "Does that mean I'm good-looking?"

She smirked, those rosy lips of her curving. "You know, in a nice-boy way."

"I'm not a dreamboat."

She drew back so their arms were no longer touching, and acted as if she were evaluating him. "Maybe you'd be a dreamboat for the right girl."

"Not you?"

She laughed, then shoved his arm. But she was blushing too. "You're nuts, Sam. You're like my . . . brother."

He knew it—of course he knew it—but hearing her say the words felt like she'd socked him in the stomach. He thought he'd kept his expression neutral, but apparently he hadn't.

"*Sam*?" Her mouth dropped open. Then she scrambled off the hammock and faced him. "Do you . . ." Her voice cut off as if she wasn't physically able to finish the question.

He was at a crossroads. He could laugh this off, say he was teasing, meant nothing by it. Or . . . he could confess. He decided to do what he'd come here for. Rising to his feet, he swallowed, then said, "Look, Susan, I need to tell you something."

She took a step back, her eyes rounded.

He folded his arms, then unfolded them and set his hands on his hips. "I'd like to take you to the Spring Fling. You don't need to worry about a new dress. You'd look beautiful in anything."

Was he talking too fast? "And I, uh, we could go as friends like we've always been. But if there's any chance you see me as something other than a buddy, or a brother"—he winced—"I wouldn't mind that either." He drew in a breath, although he wasn't sure if Susan was breathing at all. "I like you, Susan. As a friend, of course. Always have. But lately, I've realized something else. I like you more than a friend. And I have to tell you because it's been eating me up inside for a while. I want you to know the truth."

Susan didn't say anything for a long moment, but her face had gone from pink to a rather pale white, which made her freckles more pronounced. "Sam," she whispered.

"You don't have to come up with any answer right now." Deflation coursed through him. "Maybe we could talk later today. Or tomorrow. Or whenever you want."

The Healing Garden

She gave a slow nod, but didn't respond.

Sam should go, he really should. He'd shocked her enough. He bent to pick up the book that had fallen and set it on the hammock. Then he shoved his hands in his pockets and headed out of the yard. His house was only three down, and by the time he got home, his throat felt like a boulder was stuck in it.

He didn't know if it being a Saturday was good or bad. He wouldn't see her until Monday unless he went to church, and that would be really obvious. Surely she wouldn't make him wait too long, right? Even if her answer wasn't what he wanted to hear, it would at least put him out of his misery.

Because miserable was how he felt.

He headed into the house. His mom had left the windows open to let in the late winter air. He could hear a radio playing music from the kitchen and guessed she was in there getting an early start on dinner preparations. His father had taken on a second job and worked weekends, as well as his regular job during the week. It had been decided after a vigorous discussion between his parents of whether his mom should take in ironing to help their budget.

His father had finally declared that he didn't want his wife to iron another man's clothing. The statement was extreme, but it seemed the entire country was dealing with anxiety over finances, and his parents were no exception.

Sam would normally hang out in the kitchen and help his mom, but right now, he needed to get his head straightened out. And his heart. He took the stairs two at a time to his second-floor bedroom. A poster stared at him from the wall that said, "Join the Air Service. Learn-Earn."

Sam aimed to join the Air Service. He flopped onto his bed and sprawled out, propping his hands behind his head, thinking about Susan. Doubts began to plague him, and he wondered if he should have told her that he liked her.

She was his best friend, and he didn't want anything to change that. Why couldn't he have been more patient? He'd let the boys talking about the Spring Fling push him into confessing too fast. He should have waited, because he liked Susan for life, and he didn't really care about a school dance. Sure, it wouldn't be any fun seeing her go out with Jerry, or whoever else, but the silence between them was much worse.

Sam moved off his bed and paced the small room between the twin beds and single dresser. He supposed he could go talk to one of the fellas, but they'd just tell him he was an idiot. And he already knew that.

With a sigh, he headed out of his room and down the stairs.

His mother sat at the kitchen table now, peeling a few potatoes.

"Want some help?" he asked.

She waved him off. "I'm almost finished. I thought you were going to see Susan?"

"I did see her."

At the flat tone of his voice, she seemed to know things hadn't gone well. She reached to turn off the radio. "What's going on? Did you two get into a fight?"

It was kind of a humorous thing to ask since he and Susan hadn't been in a squabble since they were maybe ten years old.

"I'm not sure what it was," Sam said. "I asked her if she wanted to go to the Spring Fling with me."

"Oh?" His mother's forehead creased, and she set down the potato peeler. "That seems . . . unprecedented."

Sam dropped his gaze and ran a fingernail along a groove in the table. "It is . . . but I wanted to ask her."

His mother rested her hand on his arm. "What's going on, son? Do you want to date Susan?"

He couldn't deny it, could he, at least not to his mother. "Yes. I told her I liked her, and she . . ." He scrubbed a hand through his short hair. "She was very surprised."

"Ah." His mother folded her hands atop the table. "I thought this might happen."

He lifted his gaze. "That Susan wouldn't like me more than a friend?"

"No." She seemed to be sorting through her words. "I've noticed how you've felt about her for some time now, and it was clear she didn't catch on to that."

Sam puffed out a breath. "Is that good or bad? I mean, if she can only see me as a friend, then I'll just have to live with that. But now I've made things really awkward between us." He groaned.

His mother gave a soft chuckle.

"Is this entertaining?" he said, then immediately regretted it. "Sorry, I didn't mean to snap."

His mother rose from her chair and cleared off the potato peelings. "She'll come around, Sam, you'll see."

"What does that mean?"

"It means," she said in a quiet voice, "you're a great young man, and if she has any sense in her, she'll go on that date with you. Now that you've told her you like her, she'll start thinking in that direction. Who knows what she'll come up with."

"That's just the thing," Sam lamented. "Staying friends might be agony."

His mother smiled again. "I think you're sore right now, but tomorrow, or the next day, that will fade. Whatever happens will be the right thing. You can't force love."

Sam was sure his ears were bright red. They definitely felt hot. "Well, if you need me, or if Susan comes over, I'll be in the backyard digging something."

"Smart plan," his mother said. "Work will sort out your thoughts. While you're at it, can you edge around the fruit trees? Dad will be grateful."

Sam headed into the backyard, wondering if any amount of digging could sort out his thoughts.

Six

1919

SUSAN MADE SAM WAIT AN entire week. Sure, he'd seen her at school. She'd even said hi, but her tone and actions made it clear she wasn't open to further conversation.

Every class, every bell, every passing in the hallway was agony on Sam. How had he been such an idiot? If she wasn't even speaking to him, was there hope of keeping a friendship at all? Had he acted too early? Too impulsively? Maybe he was confused. Maybe he wasn't really in love with Susan, but they spent so much time together that he'd mixed things up.

"Sam?" his mother said outside his room just before she knocked softly on his door. "You have a visitor."

Sam immediately stiffened. He'd been slogging through his homework with a single lamp in his room, as the shadows of twilight deepened around him. He hadn't realized it was nearly ten o'clock on Friday night—which he'd spent alone. Who would be coming by this late?

There was no censure in Mother's tone.

"Who is it?" he asked, his heart climbing his throat. It was likely a couple of his buddies, stopping by to see if he wanted to join them for sodas. They would have considered it too late to call his house in case his parents were sleeping.

"Susan," his mother said.

Was it possible for a heart to suddenly stop beating, then start up again?

"All right," he somehow managed to say in a semi-normal tone. "I'll be right down." He pushed up from his desk and glanced wildly about his room. Should he change clothing? Should he rush to the bathroom and check his hair? No . . . he'd be who he was right now. He didn't need to spiff up to get rejected. He grabbed a mint from the small box on his desk. Then he was ready.

Walking down each step felt like he was descending to his doom. His life sentence. To hear the words of his judgment. His mother was nowhere to be seen, and Susan stood in the doorway of their living room, as if she was undecided if she wanted to come into the house or flee back to hers.

"Hi," he said, his voice sounding scratched.

"Hi." Susan's eyes were wide as she surveyed him. She was dressed as if she were going to a party. She wore one of her nicer dresses, and her hair was styled with finger curls. She wore low-heeled pumps that made her a couple of inches taller.

"How are you?" she said after a long moment.

Sam rubbed the back of his neck. She was here, and that was something to be grateful for, right? "I've had better weeks."

Her smile was tentative. "So have I."

Now, what did that mean? Guilt crept in. He'd ruined their friendship, so of course she was probably hating him right now. But she'd been courteous enough to come over and end it officially in person.

"I'm sorry," he ventured. "About everything. I never should have made you uncomfortable. I should have kept those thoughts to myself."

The Healing Garden

Her brow furrowed, and she stepped toward the door.

Now what had he done? Before he could apologize for apologizing, she spoke. "Do you think we could talk outside?" She glanced past him.

His parents weren't on the main floor, but that didn't mean they wouldn't be able to hear them in the quiet of the house. "Of course," he said.

Susan turned and pushed through the door, Sam following. She didn't stop on the porch, though. She continued across the front yard, then stopped under the group of trees at the corner of the property. They'd spent many afternoons lounging in the grass in the shade of these trees. Sometimes reading or playing games. Other times talking about outrageous future plans, all of which seemed laughable right now.

When Susan stopped, Sam stopped, leaving plenty of distance between them. They were back far enough from the street that if a car drove through the neighborhood, they'd stay concealed.

"Sam, I've been thinking about what you said . . ."

He folded his arms, creating some sort of protective barrier against her words and his emotions.

"And I like you too." She released a breath, as if it had been a difficult thing to say.

He knew she liked him. They were best friends—or had been.

"And if you're still asking, I want to go to the Spring Fling with you."

Now this did surprise him. "As friends?" he blurted out before he could think reasonably. She'd just raised the flag of peace and he had to question it.

She smiled then, and he knew he'd give his right arm to know what was going on inside her head right now.

"Yes, as friends," she said with a laugh.

But the laugh only pierced his chest like a hot fire poker.

"We've always been friends, Sam. Do you think that would change just because we're going steady?"

Wait... "Steady? As in going on more than one date?"

Her smile grew. "If you'll ask me. I suppose I could ask you too. I mean, it's 1919."

Sam blinked. Were Susan and her red hair and smile a mirage? Had he fallen asleep at his desk doing homework? Would he wake up in a couple of hours with a kinked neck and dry mouth?

He dragged a hand over his face, then refocused on her. "You want to go steady with me?" His voice was barely audible, but surely she heard it.

"I do." She took a small step closer to him. "If you haven't changed your mind?"

Sam laughed, mostly in surprise and relief. "I haven't changed my mind. I'd never change my mind."

"Good." Susan was grinning now. "Because I want to try something."

Race through the dark streets? Jump out of a tree? She could name it, and he'd do it.

"What do you want to—" His voice cut off when she closed the distance between him.

Placing her hands on his shoulders, she pushed up on her toes and pressed her mouth against his.

It all happened so fast, so unexpectedly, that Sam didn't react at first. She drew away, releasing him, her eyes filled with vulnerability. He was still an idiot. She'd kissed him, and he'd done nothing. Well, she was still standing there, and so was he.

Sam moved his hands to her waist and pulled her close. Then he kissed her. She was much quicker to react, and her hands returned to his shoulders. This was definitely not an expert kiss, but there were plenty of fireworks. Mostly, his skin burned at the press of her body against his, and the softness of her lips, and the all-encompassing scent of Susan.

This time, when she drew away, she didn't step out of his arms. He rested his forehead against hers. "Is that what you wanted to try?"

Her laughter was soft. "Yes."

"And what did you think?"

"Well, you're definitely not my brother."

Sam smiled. "Definitely not." Then he kissed her again.

After he walked Susan home that night, Sam wasn't sure his feet actually touched the ground as he headed back to his house. He couldn't have dreamed up a better scenario, and he'd be surprised if he slept at all that night. Or the next night, or the next.

By the time Monday afternoon rolled around, everyone at school knew they were an item. Susan had held his hand in the hallways, and Sam wasn't about to protest. His head was in the clouds, his heart was soaring, and his feet barely touched the ground. His friends teased him, but he didn't care.

Susan was going steady with him, and nothing could change his elation.

Until the night before the Spring Fling. When she showed up at his doorstep right after the dinner hour, her cheeks stained with tears, Sam ushered her onto the porch.

"What's wrong?"

"My dad lost his job this morning," Susan said. "He's been making phone calls all over the city, but there's nothing."

Sam felt like he'd been kicked in the gut. Her father had undergone more than one pay cut at work, a fact that Susan only knew because she'd overheard a conversation between her parents. They'd been economizing, like everyone had.

"But it's worse than I thought," she said in a quiet voice, her eyes focused on the porch. "I overheard my parents talking. They haven't been able to pay their mortgage for the last three months."

Sam frowned. "Oh no."

Susan gave a short nod. "We're going to be kicked out," she whispered. "The bank isn't going to keep floating us."

He swallowed hard, his mind racing. Susan had an aunt in the city, but she lived in a small apartment.

"You could live here," Sam said. "We'll make room. My parents would be happy to accommodate."

Susan lifted her chin, but her eyes were sad. "The six of us wouldn't fit. Besides, my dad's pride wouldn't allow it. My mom is making phone calls too. She might work at the bakery."

They both knew there weren't jobs at the bakery. Susan's mom might get a few hours, but that wouldn't pay a mortgage. New tears started down her cheeks, and Sam pulled her into his arms for a tight hug.

She cried against his chest for a few moments until she was able to steady her breath. "I have savings," he whispered against her ear. "And I can sell my baseball card collection."

Susan drew away and shook her head. "I'm not going to use your savings. Besides, we need a long-term solution. We'll figure something out. We just have to have faith."

Sam had to hold on to her words because the alternative was too painful to think about.

"I'll talk to my parents," he said. "Maybe my dad will have some things in mind."

Susan shrugged. "Maybe." But there was no hope in her eyes. "I don't know if I should go to the Spring Fling. It seems inconsiderate to go to a dance when my parents might be losing the house."

Sam dragged in a breath and grasped her hand. "We'll do whatever you want. Just let me know."

Her eyes glimmered with new tears as she lifted up on her toes and kissed him. Right there in front of the whole neighborhood.

Sam's heart skipped a couple of beats. He'd never get tired of Susan's kisses, or her touch.

"Thanks for understanding, Sam."

He nodded, ignoring the tight twist of regret in his stomach. The Spring Fling didn't matter. Susan and her family did. And if she felt like she needed to focus on their predicament, then dances could wait. There'd be more.

The following afternoon, Sam had mostly forgotten about the dance, since he was caught up in scouring the newspapers for job opportunities he could pass along to Susan's dad. He even called to inquire on a few, but was told the positions were no longer available.

When a knock sounded on the door, he was the one to answer it since his parents were both out of the house.

Susan stood on the porch, wearing a blue floral dress. Her eyes danced and her mouth curved in amusement at his expression.

"Surprise," she said in a light tone. "We're going to the Spring Fling."

"We are?"

She nodded. "My dad found a job." Her mouth was smiling, but her eyes glimmered with unshed tears.

"That's amazing, where?" he asked.

She hesitated, then her voice trembled as she said, "It's in Nevada, so we'll have to move. We're going to live with my uncle, and my dad's working for him."

Sam couldn't have been more shocked. "*Nevada?* When?"

She lifted a shoulder. "Soon. We'll finish out the school year there."

His mind reeled. "Maybe you can stay here to finish? It would be hard to—"

Susan stepped close and kissed his cheek. Then she took his hand. "I have to go with my family, but we'll write all the time. And we'll figure out how to see each other in the summer."

Questions raced through him, but he could see that her emotions were already on the surface. As were his. He squeezed her hand. "I'll get ready."

Seven

1981

THE MOMENT CARLY CAME THROUGH the door, Anita brushed off her hands and hurried inside the house. It was her first day back, and Anita had worried about it all day. Mostly about rumors affecting Carly and how the friend circle was doing.

"Well?" Anita asked as she set down her backpack. "How did it go?"

"Fine," Carly said as she picked out an apple from the bowl on the kitchen counter. She took a bite out of it and picked up her backpack. "I have homework."

With that, she disappeared into her bedroom.

Anita blew out a breath. She'd spent part of the day at the mechanic's having the battery replaced and everything else looked over. Then she'd come home to an empty mailbox when she was hoping one of her commission checks would show up. Next, she'd endured another phone call from Glenn, who seemed to have the day off.

She really needed to tell him that she wasn't interested.

Hearing Mr. Davis talk about his wife Norma, and then the mysterious Susan, made her realize he'd been a man who'd loved two women. One he'd lost, and the other he'd married. The softness of his tone and the tenderness in his eyes when he spoke of them told Anita that Glenn didn't hold that type of place in her heart.

The doorbell rang, and she frowned. She wasn't expecting anyone. When she opened the door to Phyllis, she pushed back the irritation. They'd already talked earlier that day over the fence in the backyard.

"Look what's come up early," Phyllis said, holding out a basket.

Sassy ran into the house, weaving between their legs, and disappeared somewhere. Likely to Carly's bed.

Anita peered into the basket. "Oh, they're carrots." They were carrots, but they were a deep orange, almost brown color. "I don't think those are early carrots, though."

Phyllis's brow pinched. "You think they're from last year?"

"I do." Anita picked up one of the carrots. It was soft in her hands. "Yes, definitely from last year."

"Oh." Phyllis looked so deflated that she said, "That's great you found them because I might be able to dry them in slices and use them in my art."

"That's so clever of you." Phyllis's entire face brightened. "I knew they'd have some use, even if they aren't edible."

Anita thought again about the "lonely" comment that Carly had made about their neighbor. "Phyllis, if you don't have dinner plans, would you like to eat with us?"

Her brows popped up. "You two go ahead. I'm on a special diet."

Anita couldn't have been more surprised. Phyllis was very trim and went on a brisk walk every day. "What sort of diet?"

"The grapefruit diet," Phyllis proudly stated. "It's a seven-day plan and promises I'll lose ten pounds. I started it yesterday."

The Healing Garden

Anita scanned the woman's face, from her gold-framed glasses to her carefully lined lips and lipstick. "You look wonderful already, Phyllis. I don't think you need to lose one pound."

The woman's cheeks flushed, which she found curious.

"You're sweet to say so." She handed over the basket. "Now, enjoy your dinner with your daughter and I'll see you tomorrow."

Anita grasped the basket of carrots. "All right. See you tomorrow."

Closing the door, she shook her head. What did Phyllis see when she looked in the mirror? When could a woman stop worrying about her appearance? Apparently not in her seventies.

Anita headed into the kitchen and set the basket of carrots on the counter. She didn't know if she'd be able to really use them, but she'd experiment.

She turned to the refrigerator and opened it, scouring the contents for a dinner idea that would decidedly not include grapefruit. She finally settled on tacos to use up the leftover chicken from the night before, but instead of calling Carly to come help with preparations, Anita turned on the television. *The Phil Donahue Show* was playing, but she didn't pay much attention. She just wanted background noise to distract her from her thoughts as she prepared dinner.

As she was shredding the cooked chicken, the phone rang. She quickly rinsed off her hands, then picked up the receiver, hoping it wasn't Glenn again. It was.

"Hello, Anita, I'm glad I caught you."

"Oh, why's that?" she asked, pushing down her irritation. She'd told herself she'd break things off with him the next time he called. But at this moment, she didn't want to deal with it.

"I'm just down the road at a gas station," he said in a cheerful tone. "What are your dinner plans?"

"Fixing dinner right now," she said, then winced. Maybe she shouldn't have said that . . .

"Ah, that sounds nice," he said. "Want company? I can bring drinks."

"I'm sorry, Glenn." She wasn't exactly sorry. "It's just me and Carly tonight. She's going through some things that need my full attention."

He was quiet for a moment. "I think you need a night off. The kid can stay on her own for a bit, or maybe she could hang out with friends. I'll take you somewhere nice."

The sentiment was probably genuine, but it irked Anita because it felt like he was overriding her parenting decisions. "That's kind of you to offer," she ground out. "And I know this isn't ideal over the phone, but I just don't think our relationship is going anywhere. I've got to focus on my daughter and career right now. I thought I'd have more time for you, but it turns out I don't. So I think we should just stay friends."

Glenn laughed.

Was this funny? Amusing?

"You're a real heartbreaker, Anita," he said sarcastically, which told her he didn't think she was a heartbreaker at all. "Just so you know, you're missing out. I don't see the men lined up at your door, so if you're turning me down, then your loneliness is your fault."

She opened her mouth to protest, but Glenn barreled on. "You're the one who flirted with me, and I wasn't too excited that you had baggage, but I was willing to stay open-minded."

"Carly isn't baggage," Anita cut in. "She's my daughter."

"Well, put yourself in my shoes," he said. "Why would I want to raise another man's kid?"

The Healing Garden

"No one has asked you to raise her," she cut in again.

"Good, because you're a cold witch, and I don't want anything to do with you or your kid."

Anita gripped the receiver, ready to deliver her own insults, but Glenn hung up.

One second, he was breathing fire at her, and the next, the line clicked off.

Anita was stunned. Glenn had gone from a gregarious, complimentary—if a bit cheesy—guy trying to get a date to a spiral of viciousness. She set the receiver in its cradle, then sank onto a kitchen chair, resting her head in her hands.

What a creep. She should be glad to be rid of him, but tears stung her eyes anyway. Dating as a single mom wasn't easy on her end, which was why she'd put it off for so long. She always had to consider Carly. But would every man think like Glenn? That she was full of baggage?

"Mom?" Anita snapped her gaze up to see Carly in the kitchen, Sassy in her arms. "What's wrong?" she asked.

Anita quickly wiped her eyes and tried to think of what Carly might have overhead. "That was Glenn. He . . . we broke things off. Not that we were doing a lot of dating anyway."

Carly smiled, petting Sassy. "Good. He smelled."

This wasn't what Anita expected at all. "What do you mean he *smelled*?"

Her daughter's nose wrinkled. "Like he used a whole bottle of cologne before he came over."

She smiled. "Yeah, he does like cologne."

Carly exaggerated rolling her eyes. "*Like* it? He must have a mail subscription that comes every week."

Anita laughed, and it felt good. "Well, I'm glad you're not heartbroken over it."

Carly scoffed. She set down the cat, then moved to the stove. "What's for dinner?"

"Oh." Anita pushed to her feet. They were changing the subject, and that was good. "Chicken tacos."

The rest of the week was fine—pleasant, in fact. Carly came home straight after school and didn't complain about being grounded. Anita made excellent progress on her projects, and she got Mr. Barton's portrait delivered.

Friday after school, Carly burst into the house. She rushed past Anita, who'd just come in from the garden, and shut herself in her bedroom.

"Carly?" she called, heading down the hallway. Sassy trotted after her and stopped in front of Carly's door. Anita paused by the door, hearing sniffling. "What's wrong?"

She heard a mumbled, "Go away."

Anita closed her eyes and leaned her head against the closed door. The school hadn't called, so it wasn't an administration problem. She hadn't gotten into trouble again, right? Then she remembered Carly had had a gnarly math test today.

"How did math go?" she asked through the door.

"Fine." Carly's tone was tight, but at least she was still speaking.

Anita released a slow breath. "Can I come in? And Sassy too?"

There was a pause, then Carly said, "If you want."

Gratitude flooded her as she turned the doorknob. At least her daughter was willing to talk. They could fix whatever this was, together.

Carly was curled on her bed, tears staining her cheeks, and this brought Anita up short.

"Oh, honey, what's wrong?"

Then she started to cry in earnest. Anita sat on the edge of her bed and wrapped her arms about her. Sassy jumped up on the bed and nudged Carly, purring. After several long moments, she was composed enough to say, "Samantha and Evie are mad at me."

Anita drew in a breath, not sure how to react. "What happened?"

Carly wiped at her cheeks, then drew away from her embrace. She scooped Sassy onto her lap and held her close. "They wanted to walk into town to get milkshakes and skip the period after lunch. I told them I couldn't skip, or I'd be grounded for longer." More tears dripped along her cheeks, and Anita handed over a tissue.

Carly dabbed at the tears. "So they left me, and when I saw them after school, I tried to say hi. But they both ignored me. Everyone was watching too, so now the whole school knows that I was ditched."

Anita's mind raced. "Wow. That was really rude of them." Was this just a tiff? Was it serious? Was it bullying?

"Honey," she said, rubbing Carly's shoulder. "If they really ditched you, then you're better off without them. Also, you can have your own opinion about things and not always have to go along with a poor choice in order to maintain a friendship."

Carly frowned. "That's such an adult thing to say."

"Well, I am an adult."

Carly's mouth lifted. "True."

Anita smiled, then sobered. "I'm really sorry they were mean to you, but I'm really proud of you too. Standing up for yourself is so important, and it doesn't end in middle school. It's just a hard thing to do when you're friends with someone who doesn't care about your well-being."

Carly's brows lifted. "They care. Or at least they did when we were friends."

Anita touched the edged of her braid. "Friendships can be complicated, no matter how old you are. But if a person doesn't care about you getting into trouble, then they aren't your real friend in the first place."

Carly bit her lip, her gaze falling. "Yeah, maybe." She rested her chin on top of Sassy's head. "What if they call me and want to be friends again?"

Anita was more than happy to tell the two girls "good riddance," but she knew Carly had to navigate this herself. "If they do call you, and if you do want to forgive them, you should still tell them you aren't going to do things that will put you in a tough spot."

Carly nodded, and she felt gratitude rush through her. Maybe her parenting skills were finally spot-on tonight.

"I think that's a good plan."

Anita smiled, but not too wide. "Okay, great. Now, are you hungry? Maybe after dinner, we could go get some ice cream?"

Carly's eyes lit up. "Okay. That would be great."

Anita tried not to do a victory jump after leaving Carly's bedroom. She hated to see her daughter in pain, but if that pain gave her more wisdom and helped her mature, then maybe it was a blessing in the end.

After dinner, when they loaded into the car and headed toward the ice cream shop, Carly said, "I guess we're both starting over."

Anita raised her brows. "What do you mean?"

"You dumped Glenn, and I have to find a new circle of friends."

She reached over and squeezed her daughter's hand. "I have no doubt you'll find those friends. What about Sara? You've done a couple of things with her—before you became friends with the others."

"Yeah, she's cool," Carly said, twisting a piece of hair around her finger. "She asked me to do something a couple weeks ago, but I already had plans."

The Healing Garden

"See?" Anita said. "You're an easy person to be a friend with. Maybe call her tonight. You can make plans for tomorrow night if you want."

"Am I done being grounded?"

"I've been thinking about that," she said. "You showed a lot of maturity sticking up for yourself today, so I think you've learned your lesson."

"Yes!" Carly pumped her fist in the air, and Anita laughed.

It felt good to be on the same page with her daughter once again.

"What about you, Mom?"

"What about me?"

"You know. Are you going to find another man to date?"

"I've never really looked," Anita said in a light tone, although her stomach felt pinched. "I'm perfectly happy with how things are right now. You're my priority, then my art comes second. A man just muddles things up."

Carly scooted down in her seat and propped her knees against the dash. "Whatever, Mom. You don't want to be a spinster forever."

"Well, maybe not forever," she said in an exaggerated voice. "But I'm not in any hurry."

Eight

MR. DAVIS WAVED A HAND from his place at a table when Anita walked into the dining room with Carly. Anita smiled as Carly increased her stride and called out, "Hello, Mr. Davis."

She wasn't sure what exactly had connected these two so quickly, but she was grateful for it. Who would have thought her daughter would be sharing her friendship woes with a war vet. But that was what happened when they were halfway through a Scrabble game.

"Have you heard of the phrase, there are friends for a season and friends for a reason?" Mr. Davis asked, pausing before he took his next turn.

"No," Carly said, tilting her head. Today she wore a high ponytail with one of the scrunchies she'd made herself. The bright pink fabric matched her nearly fluorescent pink T-shirt.

Mr. Davis's expression was somber when he replied, "You don't have to regret a friendship, even if it ends badly, or even if you're sad about it not being something more. Friendships help us grow as a person and they also teach us to be better friends down the road."

Carly's eyes brightened. "So if Evie and Samantha keep me out of their friend group, then I should be okay with it?"

"I believe so." Mr. Davis laid out the next word on the Scrabble board. "They were friends for a season, and now it's time for you to find another friend. You've outgrown the antics of skipping classes or raiding kitchens. I can tell you're a serious student, and you have a bright future to keep in mind."

He laid out the word, *petri*.

"Petri?" Carly said. "Like a petri dish?"

"Exactly," he said with a nod. "See, you're already smarter than most kids your age." He glanced over at Anita. "I'll bet your mother had good advice about your former friends."

Carly didn't hesitate. "Yeah, she said those girls aren't my real friends if they don't care about getting me in trouble."

"Your mother is a wise woman," Mr. Davis said, then threw her a wink.

Anita couldn't help but smile.

Then he started in with a story about his high school days, talking about his friends, including Susan.

It was at that moment Wyatt arrived.

Anita immediately noticed his frown at the mention of Susan. It was none of her business, not really, but it still made her wonder. Had Wyatt ever done any investigating into Susan? Maybe looked for her name in phone books? Checked old high school records?

"Hey, Gramps," he said in a friendly tone, although his eyes darted from Carly to Anita. Had there been a quick furrow of his brows? He hugged his grandpa, then settled next to him. "Looks like your favorite visitors are here."

"Ah." Mr. Davis waved a hand. "You're my favorite. Carly is a close runner-up, though."

Wyatt's smile remained in place, but there it was again. A pull of his brows. Anita hadn't imagined it after all.

Was their visit bothering him, or was it something else?

"I was just telling Carly how to navigate friendships," Mr. Davis said. "It's been a while since I was in school myself, but there are some things I'll never forget. I guess it might be unusual, especially in my day, to have a girl as a best friend. But Susan was just that."

"Yeah, that's nice, Gramps," Wyatt said, dismissing the conversation thread altogether. He slipped off his suit jacket and set it on the back of the chair before sitting down. Both times Anita had seen him, he'd been wearing a suit. Did the man never dress down before coming to visit his grandpa?

"Paula said she's coming to visit today," Wyatt said.

Mr. Davis clapped his hands together. "Wonderful. I thought she couldn't get away."

"She was able to get the day off from the hospital."

Mr. Davis looked over at Anita and Carly. "Paula is Wyatt's little sister. She's a nurse. Did I tell you that?"

"I don't think so," Anita said at the same time that Carly shook her head.

"What kind of nurse?" Carly asked.

The interest in her voice was something Anita hadn't heard before.

"She takes care of the new mothers and their babies."

"Labor and delivery," Wyatt added.

"She works most weekends, so I never see her," Mr. Davis said, not complaining, but sounding like he missed his granddaughter.

Anita wondered where the parents were—the son or daughter of Mr. Davis?

"Paula saw you last month," Wyatt said.

Mr. Davis frowned as if he were trying to remember. Then his brow relaxed, and he turned back to the Scrabble game. "Want to join us on the next round?"

"Sure," Wyatt said with a barely concealed sigh. "I'll get

The Healing Garden

some drinks." He rose and paused. "Does everyone want a drink? Punch or water?"

"Punch," both Mr. Davis and Carly said at once.

"I'll have some water," Anita said.

Wyatt tilted his head toward her. She took the hint and said, "I'll help."

As they walked toward the refreshment table together, he looked at her. "Did you ask my grandpa about Susan? Or did he start talking about her on his own?"

Anita wasn't sure how to respond at first. Was Wyatt accusing her of something? "He barely brought her up when you arrived. My daughter and I aren't asking him those types of questions."

He must have caught the defensive tone in her voice because he paused in his step. "I appreciate you spending time with Gramps. He seems to enjoy the company and playing games with someone other than me. But I don't want his false memories encouraged."

Anita didn't answer for a moment. The intensity of his green eyes told her that Wyatt wasn't just concerned his grandfather was dealing with memory loss, or false memory creation, but he was worried about something deeper.

They reached the table, and she poured a cup of punch for Carly, then looked over at him. "You know, you can find out pretty easily. Wouldn't the city library have copies of old yearbooks? Why don't you look up your grandfather's class?"

Wyatt folded his arms, a frown marring his face. "That's actually a good idea. But I don't think it's necessary."

"Because you don't think Susan is real?"

"He never mentioned her before," Wyatt said firmly. "And the postcard wasn't even addressed to him."

"What are you worried about? That she's real or that your grandfather is dealing with memory confusion?"

Wyatt glanced over at his grandfather. "Either one, I guess. He's been through a lot in life, and I don't want him hurt any more."

Anita supposed there was a lot of depth to that statement. She wondered why Wyatt thought that his grandfather's memories of an old friend would hurt him.

"I think you should find out once and for all," Anita said. "It would put your mind at rest, and you'd know how to better respond to the stories he's sharing."

"Maybe you're right," Wyatt said, studying her. "I just hate that all of his conversations turn toward a woman we've never heard about instead of my own grandmother."

"Maybe it's how he's coping?" she suggested. "Thinking of his life before he met your grandmother?"

"Maybe." Wyatt turned toward the refreshment table and gathered a plate of cookies and the rest of the drinks.

Anita walked with him back to where Carly was apparently winning in Scrabble against Mr. Davis.

When Wyatt joined in the game, it moved much faster, and Mr. Davis started laying down more complicated words. Maybe he'd been holding back in his playing with Carly.

By the time his granddaughter showed up, he had beat them all more than once.

"Hi, Gramps," Paula said, bending to kiss him on the cheek.

Anita's first impression of her was a small fireball. She laughed easily, asked a dozen questions, and teased mercifully. Her dark hair, brown eyes, and petite frame were similar to her grandfather's, making her older brother even more of an anomaly.

"I wasn't sure if you were here for Gramps or my brother." Paula gave Anita a broad smile.

She had to laugh. "We're here to visit the residents and ended up at your grandpa's table."

"Ah." Paula's eyes flashed with amusement. "I told Wyatt coming here on the weekends was no excuse not to date. He acts like he's too busy for all of that, but now that I see you, I understand why he's here two weekends in a row."

"Hey," he cut in. "I can hear you, sis. You know I try to come every weekend."

Paula grinned. "I came more than you last month, so that's not true at all." She leaned toward Anita. "He's one of those numbers guys. Stiff and boring. Doesn't even know how to flirt."

Wyatt's ears pinked, and Anita wanted to laugh, but she held back.

She guessed Wyatt to be close to her age, yet he could still get riled by his sister. And what did Paula mean he didn't know how to flirt? Had he never had a girlfriend before? She found that hard to believe. He was articulate, handsome, hygienic, and although he seemed a bit opinionated, he was well-mannered as far as she could tell.

She'd also caught him watching her more than once. Not that she could read his expression or decipher his thoughts, but she didn't think he was someone to back down from a challenge. Which meant if he was interested in a woman, surely he'd pursue her.

"I'd rather not be known as a lady's man," Wyatt told his sister. "We can't all be flirty like you or no one would ever be in a serious relationship. Which means that neither of us would exist."

"You're such a sweet talker," Paula said. "When you're not literal about everything."

"Don't make me sit between the two of you," Mr. Davis said. "You're setting a bad example for the kid at our table."

Anita didn't mind the banter between the siblings, and she noticed that her daughter was soaking it all in. After another round of Scrabble, with Carly beating everyone, it was finally time to go.

"I'll walk you two out," Paula said, pushing up from the table.

After saying goodbye to both Mr. Davis and Wyatt, they headed out of the dining room. Paula looped her arm with Anita's.

"Thanks so much for spending time with Gramps," she gushed. "He's tickled that you'd play games with him. He doesn't get any other visitors."

"It's been fun," Anita said. "And as long as Carly wants to keep coming, I'll keep bringing her." She paused. "If that's all right with you and your brother."

"It's wonderful." Paula squeezed her arm. "Now, just ignore Wyatt's fussiness. He always overthinks things, and I think it's fine if Gramps's mind wanders a bit."

"Do you think Susan is real?" Carly asked suddenly.

Paula bit her lip. "I'm not sure, but I'm surprised my brother hasn't launched an all-out investigation yet."

"What would be the downside if Susan was real?" Anita asked.

Paula released her arm as they reached the outer doors. "Wyatt was really close to Grandma, so I think he sees it as a nuisance. Or maybe even a betrayal."

"Well, either Susan was real or she wasn't," Anita said. "It might give you and your brother peace of mind to know once and for all."

Paula nodded. "I agree. Thanks again for visiting Gramps." She hugged both of them, then waved them off.

Anita and Carly headed outside into the cooling evening air. The sun had nearly set, the sky darkening with deepening twilight.

As they climbed inside the Bug, Carly said, "I like Mr. Davis."

The Healing Garden

Happiness swelled inside of Anita, who was pleased her daughter had found so much value in visiting the assisted living home. "Me too." She started the car, but the ignition only clicked, then nothing.

She released the clutch, then pushed it in again. Turning the key, she whispered, "Please start. Please start."

Nothing.

"The parking lot's flat," Carly observed, otherwise sounding nonplussed that they were once again faced with a dead car.

"The battery is brand new," Anita complained. If it was another issue, then that would just be more expensive.

She opened the door and climbed out, surveying the parking lot. Carly was right. There wasn't a slope or hill in sight.

"I'll check with the front desk to see if any of the employees have jumper cables."

"Okay." Carly climbed out of the car too, but seemed content to wait in the parking lot.

Anita hurried inside. Paula was still in the front lobby, chatting with one of the employees. "Did you change your mind?" she asked. "Want a rematch in Scrabble?"

"Our car won't start." Anita glanced from the employee to Paula. "Do you happen to have jumper cables?"

"No," she said, "but Wyatt should. He's like a Boy Scout in everything. Always prepared. I'll be right back."

"Oh, I could ask him . . ." Anita started, but Paula had already headed toward the dining room.

A moment later, Wyatt strode out, his gaze landing on her. "The battery?"

"I had a new battery put in last week," she said. "So I don't know what's going on."

He only nodded and moved past her, pushing through the front doors. "Can I see the keys?"

She handed them over and watched as he slid into the front seat. He tried to start the car, but no such luck.

"There's nothing, not even any lights coming on," he observed. Then he popped the hood and climbed out. "Do you have a flashlight?" He rolled up the sleeves of his dress shirt.

She sorted through the jockey box. "No."

Wyatt continued with his inspection. "The battery is hooked up fine," he said. "Might be something else, like the starter. It will have to be towed to a repair shop."

Dollar signs seemed to float in front of Anita's eyes. "All right. I'll go inside and call a towing service."

Wyatt straightened from the car. "I can get you both home after the towing service gets here."

"Oh, I don't want you to have to wait," she said.

He closed the hood of the car. "You'll need a ride home anyway."

"No luck?" Paula asked, crossing to them.

"We need to call a tow truck," Wyatt said.

"I can call Jimmy," Paula said. "He owes me a favor."

"Jimmy?" Anita asked.

"Her boyfriend," Wyatt said. "Unless you're *just friends* right now."

Paula flashed a saucy smile. "We're currently dating. I'll go call him, and he'll take care of all of this."

Before Anita could ask any questions, Paula hurried back into the center. "That's really nice of her, and generous of you both."

"It's no trouble," Wyatt said, and he seemed sincere. "Let's say goodbye to Gramps, then we can be on our way."

Nine

ANITA DID NOT EXPECT WYATT and Paula to be so helpful. Not only contacting the towing company, but offering a ride home as well? It was nice, though, and she wasn't going to complain. As they walked into the lobby together, she asked him, "Are we putting you out too much?"

"It's no problem," he said in a no-nonsense tone. "Paula will wait for the tow truck, and I'll take you and Carly home."

The next moments were a blur as Wyatt told his grandfather goodbye, and Paula got their phone number, then said she'd have Jim call them with an update as soon as he had one. Next thing Anita knew, she and Carly were climbing into Wyatt's car, which happened to be a shiny red Cadillac.

"This is fancy," Carly said from the back seat.

"It was Gramps's car before he couldn't drive it anymore. He and my grandma bought it right off the showroom floor in 1961." Wyatt adjusted the vents. "Too cold? Too hot?"

"It's fine." Anita glanced about the pristine upholstery. "This car looks brand new. I can't believe it's over twenty years old."

"Gramps babied it," Wyatt said, firing up the engine. "Now where to?"

"We're on Locust Street," Anita said. "Your grandfather

did an amazing job with this car. "I wish the Bug looked this good."

He cast her a smile. "Maybe when you retire and have more time on your hands, you can spend every day polishing and buffing."

"That will be the day," she said with a laugh. "I'll probably never retire since I have no pension or 401(k)."

Wyatt nodded. "I guess being self-employed has its pros and cons."

"What's your job, Mr. Davis?" Carly asked.

"Wyatt—please call me Wyatt," he said. "As much as I love my grandpa, I don't want to be called Mr. Davis." He paused, glancing in the rearview mirror at Carly. "I'm an accountant for a couple of corporations."

Anita could hear the frown in Carly's voice when she asked, "What do you do there?"

"I keep the books, attend meetings, print out reports, that sort of thing."

It all sounded interesting and gave Anita a little insight into Wyatt's personality. She wondered if he felt cooped up spending every day dealing with numbers. His shirtsleeves were still rolled up, making him look the most casual she'd ever seen him.

"Do you have a 401(k)?" Carly asked.

"Carly—" Anita started to say.

"It's all right," Wyatt said with a chuckle. "I do, in fact. Corporate America and all that. Insurance benefits with dental and vision."

"Oh, that must be nice," Carly said wistfully.

Anita turned to look at her daughter, mostly to give her a stern look to stop this line of conversation.

"We have to pay out-of-pocket for the dentist," Carly continued, completely oblivious to Anita's stare-down.

The Healing Garden

"Which is why my mom is so hyper about us brushing our teeth and flossing."

"Those are good things to do no matter what," Wyatt said, clearly amused.

"You know, Carly, we don't need to tell Wyatt all of our secrets."

"I won't tell a soul." He winked at Anita. "That's what I like about teenagers—they keep things real."

She couldn't remember the last time anyone had winked at her. And was Wyatt complimenting her daughter? What was it with the Davis family? They didn't seem to have any reservations around her or Carly.

"Oh, you should turn here, it's a shortcut," Carly said.

Anita blinked. She hadn't even been paying attention to their route. In a few moments, they'd be at the house. Should she invite him in for refreshment? Maybe offer some money for gas? How did she repay this favor?

They passed the middle school. "Is this your school?" Wyatt asked.

"Yeah," Carly said. "It's a nightmare."

Anita's mouth dropped open, and he said, "What? Why's that?"

Apparently he wasn't as shocked as she was.

"Oh, I just got into the worst friend group, and now those girls have ostracized me."

It seemed her daughter wasn't shy about holding back information from a near-stranger. Granted, that stranger was driving them home and would now know where they lived, but still . . . Carly was surprising her more and more.

"Ah, friendships as a kid can be tricky," Wyatt said. "I take that back. Friendships as an adult aren't all that much easier. You never know who you'll connect with or who will actually have your back."

"Your grandpa told me there are friends for a reason and friends for a season," Carly said.

Wyatt glanced in the rearview mirror again. "Sounds like something he'd say. I'd have to agree. Choosing your friends wisely is perhaps the most, well, wise thing you can do in life."

"Yeah, I guess I'm learning it the hard way."

"Not that I know you or your mom all that well, Carly," Wyatt said, turning at the next corner, "but you seem like a great kid. Anyone would be lucky to have you as a friend. Those other girls just lost something good, but maybe it will be better for you in the long run."

This was totally a lecture, but by the look on Carly's face, she was soaking it all in.

"Yeah, that's basically what my mom said too."

Wyatt glanced over at Anita with a smile, and she ignored the growing warmth in her chest.

"Then your mom's a smart lady."

"I guess so."

Anita laughed. "I can only speak from experience, and I loved what your grandfather said. He's full of great wisdom and has been a good friend to both of us already."

Wyatt nodded. "He talks about both of you during every phone call we have."

"It's the one with the blue shutters," Anita said as he pulled onto their street.

Wyatt slowed the car, then turned into their driveway. He shifted into park. "Thanks for spending time with Gramps. He really appreciates it, and both my sister and I do too. As you've probably surmised, I've been really swamped with work, and Paula only visits a couple times a month."

"It's been fun," Carly piped up.

"We've enjoyed every moment," Anita added. "He's a great man and full of interesting stories."

"Yeah, like Susan," Carly said. "His lost girlfriend."

Anita drew in a breath. How would Wyatt react? He hadn't been happy with all the talk about Susan—who he didn't even think was real.

"About that... Susan may or may not be a real person," he said.

"Really? Why not?" Carly sounded surprised.

"Gramps has some memory problems, and I don't really want to encourage any false memories."

"Can't we just ask someone who knew him when he was younger?" Carly suggested. "I mean, he's not that old and he probably still has some friends around he knew in high school."

Anita felt Wyatt's gaze on her, but she wasn't going to get in the middle of this.

"Your mom suggested digging through old high school yearbooks," he said. "I don't know what became of the ones belonging to Gramps, but the library probably has an archive."

"Can we go with you?" Carly asked, practically bouncing in her seat.

"Oh, we can't do that," Anita said immediately.

"I don't see why not," Wyatt said. "If I go alone, I might chicken out."

Anita didn't know what to say. Well, she should say no. This was becoming too involved, and why would Wyatt want them along on his sleuthing trip?

"What about tomorrow?" he asked.

"Libraries are closed on Sundays," Carly said.

"Oh right." His gaze shifted to Anita. "Monday or Tuesday?"

When she didn't answer right away, Carly grasped her shoulder. "Mom, please? It will be fun, and then we can make photocopies and show them to Mr. Davis."

Maybe there wasn't any harm to this plan. Mr. Davis would certainly love to see parts of his old yearbook again. And she was curious about whether Susan was a real person. "All right. I think Monday is fine. Unless you have too much homework?"

"I'll get as much done as I can tomorrow," Carly gushed. "Thanks, Mom! Now you guys need to exchange numbers."

Anita wasn't going to read any further into this situation with Wyatt because this was basically a research trip. She sifted through her purse to locate her small address book. She pulled it out, noticing the worn edges. "All right, what's your phone number, Wyatt?"

He rattled it off, then she gave him hers, which he scrawled across the back of a receipt he pulled out from his wallet.

"How about I call you Monday afternoon when I know what time I can leave work for the day?" he said. "And whatever your car situation, I'll plan on picking you up. It's only fitting we take Gramps's car on this excursion."

Anita had nearly forgotten about her car problems and how on Monday, she'd probably be facing a large repair bill. "Sounds good," she said, before she could let her thoughts send her into stress mode.

"I'll be home by three thirty," Carly said, "so any time after that works. Or my mom can check me out earlier."

Wyatt smiled. "No need for that. I usually can't get out of my office any earlier than four o'clock."

"Well, thanks again," Anita said, reaching for her door handle.

He popped out of the car, and hurried around it to fully open her door.

"Thank you," Anita said, pleased by his chivalry. He was just dropping them off—this wasn't a date or anything.

The Healing Garden

Next, he opened the door for Carly, who'd happened to wait.

"Thanks again," Anita said, wondering how many times she could thank someone in one night.

"Don't forget to call my mom," Carly said as she headed to the front porch. The light was off, and beyond the window was darkness.

Next door, the living room light glowed in Phyllis's house, and Anita thought she saw the front window curtains move. She hid a sigh. Her neighbor was probably watching.

She gave Wyatt a half-smile and turned to go.

When his hand touched her arm, she turned, surprised. "Wait," he said in a low tone. "Are you sure you're okay with this? I mean, I know Carly is gung-ho, but I don't want to intrude on your schedule."

"I think it would be great to find out once and for all, but you're the one who has to be okay with it. Not me." She paused. "You weren't too thrilled earlier tonight."

"I know." He exhaled. "But I've changed my mind, and I'm okay with it."

"Mom, I need the keys," Carly called from the front porch.

"Hang on," she said. Wyatt's gaze was still on her. "Monday, then?"

He gave a single nod. "Monday."

She turned toward the house again, and this time he didn't stop her. He didn't move either, but was apparently waiting for them to get their front door unlocked.

After opening the door and turning on the porch light, Carly bounded inside. Anita turned one more time toward the driveway.

Wyatt lifted a hand and then headed back to the car.

The light in Phyllis's living room window turned off. So

she had been watching and might be now. Anita waved toward her house just in case. If she waved back, Anita didn't know.

She headed into the house and shut the front door. She wasn't going to peer out the curtained window to watch him drive away. No. Because she wasn't going to be nosy like Phyllis.

She walked into the kitchen, where Carly stood in front of the open refrigerator.

"Hungry?" Anita asked. They could make something simple like hoagies with deli meat and cheese.

"Yeah."

"Want a hoagie sandwich?"

"Sure." Carly moved to the cupboard and pulled out the bag of hoagie bread. "I think he likes you."

"What are you talking about?"

"Wyatt Davis." Carly opened the bread bag and pulled out two buns. "He kept looking at you and smiling."

He hadn't been . . . had he? Anita was grateful that the cool air of the refrigerator was keeping her from blushing. "I don't even know him. I mean, his grandfather is a nice man, but Wyatt could be married or have a girlfriend."

"He's not, and you know that." Carly opened the rolls, laying them flat. Next she fished a knife out of the utensil drawer, then picked up the mayo jar Anita had set on the counter. "He's your age, and he's single, and he kept smiling at you. He likes that we're friends with his grandpa or he wouldn't have invited us to the library. And he's picking us up in his car instead of meeting us there. So it's like a date— except with your kid coming along."

Anita shook her head and carried the lettuce to the sink to rinse it off. "None of that means he *likes* me. He's just a nice guy and wants to help out his grandpa, so he's grateful we've been spending time with him."

The Healing Garden

Carly scoffed. "I thought adults were smarter."

Anita turned from the sink and grabbed a paper towel to pat the lettuce dry. "Believe me, I'd know if a man were trying to flirt with me, and Wyatt Davis wasn't doing that. Besides, I don't really want to date anyone for a while. I'm going to focus on you and my job."

Carly wrinkled her nose. "That's so boring, Mom. What are you going to think about all day?"

"What do you mean? I have plenty to think about."

"I don't mean listening to the radio, then talking to the neighbors about the news. That's boring too."

Anita set her hands on her hips and faced her daughter. "You know, sometimes boring is perfect. It's peaceful. It's being grateful. It's savoring the small things."

Carly shrugged. "I guess."

"Besides, I can't wait to go to the library and see if there are any new books on tape."

"Mom! You can't be serious. I know you're totally into Wyatt Davis."

Anita laughed. "Nice try, Carly. Sometimes a woman just looks forward to a good book to read."

Ten

"I CAN HELP YOU WITH those," Anita offered to Phyllis when she saw her lugging in grocery bags.

She had been trimming a few plants in the front flower bed, Sassy following her about the yard, when Phyllis pulled up. Carly was in the house doing homework, or else Anita might have brought her along to help too.

"Oh, that would be wonderful," Phyllis sing-songed. She looked as immaculate as ever. Lipstick in place, hair colored and coiffed, matching outfit of baby blue.

Anita turned off the garden hose and walked across the lawn to Phyllis's driveway. The air smelled fresh from the light morning rain and the dewy rose bushes that lined the front of her neighbor's house. Anita grabbed a couple of the bags from her trunk. Apparently the grapefruit diet was now over? Because although the bags were heavy, they looked like regular groceries.

Walking into Phyllis's house, she was struck anew at the tidiness of the place, though she'd been inside before, of course. She supposed that with only one person at home and not having art projects always in the works, housekeeping was simpler.

"Just set the bags on the counter," Phyllis instructed. "I'll unpack everything. Thanks."

Her tone was bright as usual, but something nagged

The Healing Garden

Anita in the back of her mind. Phyllis's smile was too wide, her voice too peppy, her insistence that Anita leave right away unusual. Any other time she had helped with a similar task, Phyllis had invited her to sit and chat. Have a drink or a treat.

"Is everything all right?" Anita hovered next to the counter.

"Of course," Phyllis said immediately. "I don't want to keep you waiting any longer since I know how busy you are."

Normally, she would take the out. But still she lingered. "I haven't seen your son around much lately. Are he and his wife doing well?"

This question brought a flush to Phyllis's cheeks, and Anita swore she saw a sheen of unshed tears.

Phyllis waved a hand. "Oh, they're all extremely busy right now. I haven't seen them in a few weeks, but I'm hoping when summer starts, they'll want to visit Grandma's house."

"Of course they will," Anita soothed. "If you aren't busy tomorrow, maybe we could share a quick lunch together? I need to force myself to take breaks, and that will be a good excuse."

"That would be wonderful," Phyllis said. "How about I fix something, so you don't have to worry about it. I have a house full of groceries now."

"I didn't mean to invite myself—" Anita started.

"Don't be silly." Phyllis waved a manicured hand. "If I were a better neighbor, I'd have invited you in the first place."

"You're a great neighbor," Anita said, and realized she absolutely meant it.

A short time later, as she headed back to her house, she decided that the weekend had been better than she could have ever expected—besides her car issues, that was. But then again that had been a catalyst for what was happening in a short time. Wyatt should be arriving soon to pick them up.

When she entered the house, Carly was standing at the front window. "I was just helping Phyllis with her groceries," Anita said.

Carly nodded. "I'm watching for Wyatt and the red Cadillac."

"Wow, excited?"

"As excited as you."

Anita laughed. She didn't mind Carly's teasing about Wyatt. It was good to be teasing each other and not have the tension of the suspension and grounding hanging over them. Maybe they'd get back to doing their weekend road trips, something they used to enjoy together. Today, she had been worried most of the time, wondering how Carly's school experience would go. But she came home with a smile on her face, saying she'd talked to some other girls in her classes. Maybe Samantha and Evie would be history—and that would be a good thing.

"All right, you keep watch." Anita headed out of the living room.

"He's here!" Carly called out suddenly.

She stopped. "Okay, I need to grab my purse."

"I'll see you outside."

Anita grabbed her purse, then followed Carly, locking the door behind them. When she turned, Wyatt was out of the car, wearing what he must have at work. Button-down shirt, tie, and slacks.

"Ready?" he asked, a smile playing at the corner of his mouth.

"Ready," Carly announced brightly. She hurried to the

car, splashing through a small puddle, then stopped as Wyatt opened the rear door for her.

Anita kept her stride at a normal pace, not wanting to seem too eager, even though she was probably just as keyed up.

Wyatt remained by the car, watching her approach.

Something was different about him, Anita decided. His green eyes seemed lighter in the afternoon sun, and he seemed to be more relaxed. Had it been a good workday for him?

"How are you?" he asked as she neared.

Something about his mellow voice warmed her chest. It was as if he were truly interested in her answer.

"It was a good day," she said, "once I found out Carly had a good day at school."

He paused with his hand on the door handle. "Is she making new friends?"

"She is."

He smiled. "Good to hear." He popped open the door, and she stepped past him and slid into the front passenger seat.

He smelled of fresh air and the warm sun and maybe starch. Did he starch his shirts, or was that from the dry cleaner's? She decided not to dwell on the fact that she'd spritzed a little perfume when she was getting ready.

After he climbed in and started the engine, Carly said, "This car looks shinier today than it did on Saturday. Did you wash it again?"

"No, but the sunlight brings out the true color," Wyatt said, glancing back at her. "Did you have a good day at school?"

"Pretty good," Carly said. For the next several moments, she rattled off a few conversations she'd had. "Mr. Davis will be happy that I took his advice."

"What advice was that?" Anita asked. Why didn't she know about this?

"He told me to talk to three people I hadn't before," Carly said. "He gave me some questions to ask, and well, it worked. I have new friends."

"What questions?" Wyatt asked.

That was what Anita wanted to know too.

"If they grew up here," Carly said. "Ask about the teachers they like, and then ask if they're into music and what kind." She paused. "Mr. Davis said to always have topics for conversation, even if you have to write them down and memorize them. He said people like to talk about themselves, and all you have to do is ask the questions."

Anita smiled. "That's pretty smart of him."

"I didn't realize Gramps had a method that he used," Wyatt said. "It makes sense, though. Whenever I've gone anywhere with him, he strikes up conversations with people. He doesn't care who the person is, he just talks to them, and pretty soon, they find things they have in common."

"It's a gift," Anita said. "I don't think I could do it."

Carly cut in. "Mr. Davis said it takes practice. And preparing your questions. You should try it, Mom."

"Okay . . . Do I need that sort of help?"

"Yes," Carly said immediately. "I mean, you're not friends with the moms of my friends. And they all do stuff together."

She bit her lip. Was Carly talking about her old friends, or her new friends—whom she didn't even know yet. And she couldn't do lunch dates or tennis matches with the other women because she had to work and support—

"I think Gramps had great advice," Wyatt said. "We should all try it."

"On each other?" Carly asked.

The Healing Garden

"Sure," he said. "I can start."

Everyone went silent, waiting for his question.

"So, Carly, how was school today?"

"Nooo . . ." she said. "It has to be something that doesn't have a one-word answer."

Wyatt chuckled. "Okay, okay. Carly, what do you hope we find at the library?"

"Oh, that's a good one." She leaned forward in her seat. "I hope we find out who Susan really was and more about what high school was like when Mr. Davis went. I think it will be fun to tell him what we learned." She tapped Anita's shoulder. "Your turn, Mom."

Anita cleared her throat. "All right. I'll ask Wyatt a question." He glanced over at her, a half-smile on his face. "What was your favorite part about work today and what was your least favorite?"

He tugged at his collar. "Are you sure this isn't a job interview?"

She smiled, and Carly giggled.

"Uh, today the best part was finishing a report that's taken three days to compile," he said. "The least favorite part was getting a flat tire on the way to work."

"Oh no, this car?"

"Yeah. This is my second shirt of the day and second pair of pants. What I originally wore is at the cleaner's, and I can only hope they'll get the road oil out of it."

"Road oil? What's that?" Carly asked.

Wyatt's expression went grim. "It's when you pull over to change a tire, not realizing you've stopped a few feet from a large puddle of rainwater, and the oncoming car doesn't slow down at all."

"Oh wow!" she squealed. "You got drenched?"

"I got drenched," he confirmed.

Anita couldn't help it, she had to laugh. Carly was already laughing, and within seconds, Wyatt's expression relaxed, and he laughed too.

"All right," he said, pulling onto the main road leading to the library, "it wasn't funny at the time, but I can see how it's funny later."

When they all sobered, Carly said, "It's my turn. And I'm asking you a question, Mr. Davis."

"Wyatt."

"Okay, Wyatt." She paused. "Have you lived here all your life and how old are you?"

"Carly," Anita said, "it's not polite to—"

"It's all right, Anita," he said, amusement in his tone as he patted her hand.

She froze at his touch, not knowing if she should react or ignore it. He removed his hand just as quickly as he'd touched her, so she released a slow breath. It wasn't like she had tingles running up her arm from his touch or there was some sort of electricity sparking between them like she'd read in a few books. This was different, though . . . she was *aware* of him. Of how one hand gripped the steering wheel, how the other worked the gear shift when needed, how he smelled of fresh air and starch, how he had a five o'clock shadow on his jaw, how—

"I'm forty-one, which I know makes me an old man, and I've lived in Seattle my whole life. In fact, I've only been to a couple of other states—Oregon and Nevada. So you could say that I'm a diehard Seattle-ite?"

So he was six years older than her, Anita calculated.

"My mom's thirty-five," Carly declared.

"Barely thirty-five." She wanted off that topic as soon as possible. "Don't you like to travel?"

Before he could answer, Carly cut in. "Road trips are the best! My mom and I do them all the time."

Except for the last few months, that had been the case.

"Road trips . . ." Wyatt mused as he turned into the library parking lot. "All of my traveling has been for work meetings. Once it was for a funeral of a relative. Otherwise, my grandparents didn't leave Seattle on account of my grandma's poor health."

Anita was fully curious now, with more questions. True to Carly's nature, she beat her to it.

"What was wrong with your grandma?" she asked. "And why didn't you just go somewhere with your parents?"

Wyatt pulled into a parking place and shifted the car into park.

"That's a lot of personal questions, Carly," Anita said.

He turned toward her. "It's fine." His green eyes were steady, not annoyed. "My grandma had a heart condition, so Gramps didn't want to take her too far from home—or overnight somewhere. She had trouble sleeping when she wasn't in her own bed." He paused. "And my parents . . . well, my dad took off before I could even remember him, and my mom . . . She had an addiction that eventually took her life."

Anita's heart felt like it was being twisted out of her chest. "I'm so sorry, Wyatt," she whispered.

Not even Carly had words.

"It was all a long time ago," he said gently. "Gramps and Grammy raised me, so if I seem overbearing around Gramps, you'll know why. He's everything to me."

Anita blinked against the stinging in her eyes. She wanted to hug this man, but it wasn't the right place.

"That really sucks," Carly said.

Anita normally would have reprimanded her for using such a coarse word, but right now, it was completely accurate.

"My dad left us too," Carly continued. "My mom will

try to correct me that he left her, but it was really *us*. I haven't heard from him in years, and I know he doesn't care enough about me to change that. So my mom is everything to me."

The tears came then. How had she not known that Carly felt that way? About her dad? About her? About all of it? She wiped at her cheeks, then reached over the seat to grasp Carly's hand. "You're everything to me too, sweetheart."

Wyatt didn't interrupt their moment, and only when their tears had dried did he get out of the car and open both of their doors. Anita stepped out, thanked him, then pulled Carly into a tight squeeze. They walked into the library with Wyatt leading the way.

Surprisingly, it seemed busy. A senior group must have it as their activity night because there were at least a dozen elderly people milling about. One older man, leaning heavily on a black cane, was speaking to a librarian, much louder than the "Keep Quiet" sign indicated might be acceptable. The man's white flyaway hair and deep wrinkles told her he had to be nearing ninety.

"I can't pull out those little cards from the card catalog," he was saying. "My fingers are too stiff."

The librarian murmured something, and the man said, "Speak up, I can't hear you."

Anita smiled at the interaction.

"I don't know where to start," Wyatt said, looking about the space. "Is there a sign on one of the aisles that says 'Old Yearbooks'?"

"Maybe over here?" Carly pointed to one labeled "Seattle History."

"It's as good of a place to start as any." Wyatt flashed her a smile. Then he lowered his voice even more. "Maybe

The Healing Garden

after the librarian is finished helping that gentleman, we can ask her for help if we don't find anything."

"You'll be waiting a while," a woman said, passing close to them.

Anita looked over to see an elderly woman with hair silver-white. She wore a pale yellow blouse with a jeweled brooch at the center of the collar. Everything about her bespoke elegance, from the way she angled her head, to her steady blue-green gaze, and the soft scent of roses about her.

The woman smiled conspiratorially. "Herb has been talking to the librarian since we arrived half an hour ago. He does this every trip."

Anita smiled. "Oh that's . . . interesting. And no one complains?"

The woman shrugged. "We've all learned to fend for ourselves in here. I've become a sort of expert, so if you need help, maybe I can guide you in the right direction?"

"That would be wonderful," Wyatt said. "I'm Wyatt Davis, and these are my friends and research assistants, Anita and Carly."

"Nice to meet you all," the woman said. "I'm Maggie Howard. Are you local to the area?"

All of them nodded.

Maggie sighed. "I've lived here for decades, and I've been coming to the library just as long."

"Do you check out books on tape?" Carly asked. "That's what my mom does. She's an artist, so she listens while she works."

Maggie's eyes seemed to lighten. "An artist? How wonderful. I've been collecting art most of my life. In fact, that's why I'm here."

"To collect art?" Carly asked, clearly confused like Anita was.

"No." Maggie chuckled. "I'm looking for an artist. Orlando Gallo. Have you ever heard of him? Perhaps artists are all connected?"

The hope in the older woman's voice was unmistakable.

"Orlando Gallo . . ." Anita repeated, sorting through any memories of an artist with that name. Nothing came to mind immediately. "His name isn't familiar. Is he from Seattle?"

"No," Maggie said, sounding dejected. "He's from San Francisco. I knew him many years ago." Her gaze sharpened. "Now. What are you on the hunt for today? I'm sure your adventure is much more interesting than mine."

Before she or Wyatt could answer, Carly spilled out all the information. Starting with her suspension in school, then her service hours at the assisted living home, meeting Mr. Davis, and his high school sweetheart Susan. "We don't know if she's real, though," she said, her voice nearly breathless with talking so fast.

Maggie Howard didn't seem to have any trouble following, though. Her eyes had widened as if she was hanging on every word.

"So we're going to find old yearbooks." Carly glanced at Wyatt. "From 1918 or 1919."

"From 1919." He smiled at Maggie. "Maybe you can point us in the right direction?"

She set a hand on her hip, a couple of stunning rings on her hand catching the light. "I think you were heading in the right direction. There's also a section on education a couple of aisles down from Seattle History. I can help you look too."

"Oh, we don't expect that," Anita hurried to say.

Maggie gave an exaggerated look to where Herb was still talking to the librarian. "I don't mind. I could use the distraction anyway. I've become discouraged in my search, and I think the only recourse is to take a trip to San Francisco myself."

"You'd go that far just to track down an artist?"

Maggie's smile was soft. "He used to be a friend, although we didn't know each other for too long. We lost touch, and well . . . I'd like to find him."

"Just like Mr. Davis wanting to find Susan," Carly said.

"Gramps hasn't said anything like that," Wyatt cut in, his tone firm. "We're just finding out information on *our* end."

Anita set a hand on Carly's shoulder. "Right. We don't want to encourage anything extra with Wyatt's grandfather."

"All right," she said dejectedly. Then she seemed to shrug it off. "I can't wait to see what the old yearbooks look like. The hairstyles are going to be amazing."

"Right you are, young lady," Maggie said with a chuckle.

As they walked over to the Seattle History section, Wyatt and Carly strode ahead.

Maggie fell into step with Anita. "You have a great girl, there. Now, I noticed neither you nor the gentleman you arrived with are wearing wedding rings. Is Wyatt your special someone?"

"Oh no," she said. "We've only recently met, and since Carly and I became friends with his grandfather, it sort of extended to Wyatt too. There's nothing, uh, between us."

Maggie smiled. "Friendships are very important in life. I should know. I've had over ninety years of experience. And Wyatt seems like a good man. I have a sense for these things."

Warmth prickled along Anita's arms. "You're in your nineties?"

"Ninety-four," she said with pride. "When you're my age, you wear it like a badge of honor."

"Mom!" Carly whispered-yelled. "We found the yearbooks."

Anita and Maggie shared an eager expression, then joined the others in the aisle. Carly was right. An entire section was taken up with yearbooks. Wyatt had crouched down, exploring the titles on the bottom row.

"The oldest one here is from 1952," he said, then straightened. "Maybe they have older ones on microfilm?"

"Let's ask the librarian," Maggie said. "I'll drag her away from Herb if I have to."

Wyatt's face twisted with amusement. "Do you need help?"

Her eyes twinkled. "I've got this." She moved out of the aisle, and Anita and the others followed. They stopped a few paces from where Herb was still talking to the librarian.

"Herb, I think Gerald could use your help," Maggie said. "He's been standing in front of the mystery novels for twenty minutes. Don't you know all of the detective series?"

Herb turned his eyes on Maggie, his hand gripping his cane. "I sure do. Where is Gerald?"

"Just over there." She pointed.

After Herb shuffled off, Maggie turned to the librarian, who frankly looked relieved. "Mrs. Proctor, we need some assistance," she said. "Is the microfilm room available?"

Mrs. Proctor tucked a stray bit of auburn hair behind her ear. "Of course, come this way. What are you looking for?"

Wyatt explained about the yearbooks, and she gave a brisk nod. "Just give me a few minutes, and I should be able to locate those couple of years."

They crowded into the microfilm room, and everyone took a chair. When the librarian returned, she carried a film canister. "This one has five years' worth, so you should be able to find what you're looking for—if it's here." She loaded the machine and showed everyone how to advance the images to search through the yearbook pages.

The Healing Garden

Wyatt sat in the middle chair and began to scroll through. They first found Samuel Davis listed in the index, and Carly wrote down all the page numbers to check. Finding Susan's name was harder because they didn't know her last name. There were several Susans, and who knew if there would be pictures with both Mr. Davis and Susan together anyway?

"The index might not have every mention of a person," Maggie mused. "There could be group shots of things like socials and dances."

Wyatt turned to look at her. "I remember one of his stories was about the Spring Fling."

Carly clapped her hands. "That's probably it. Hopefully there are pictures."

He continued to scroll. A page appeared with group pictures. The larger the group, the harder it was to make out faces. Some of them had identifying names at the bottom. Others didn't. When they landed on a couple of pictures from the Spring Fling, Wyatt examined them, trying to look for a young man who looked like his grandfather.

"There," he pointed. "I think that's him."

Everyone leaned closer.

Sam Davis as a young man had slicked-back hair, wore a blazer and tie, and he had his arm around a girl with short bobbed hair and a wide smile. He wasn't looking at the camera though. He was looking at his date as if the sun rose and set with her.

"Is that Susan?" Carly asked. "It has to be her."

Anita's heart stuttered. If this was Susan at Sam's side, then she was definitely real. What was Wyatt feeling right now?

He blew out a breath. "Let's see if we can match her up with pictures of the other Susans." He used the machine to print off a copy of the page with the Spring Fling photo. A few moments later, Wyatt had Carly hold it up as he scrolled to the page numbers that correlated with the girls named Susan.

"That looks like her," Carly said when he arrived at a page with a photo captioned "Glee Club."

Wyatt held the printed page close to the microfiche screen. There was no doubt it was a match.

"Susan Martin," he said. "It looks like she was a real person."

No one spoke for a couple of moments, then Carly said, "What's a glee club?"

Maggie had the answer. "A choir run by the students. It was an extracurricular club, so it was volunteer and not part of classes."

Wyatt selected the option to print off the glee club page. "We might as well find the other photos of her, as well as those of Gramps."

As the printer rattled away, he stared for a long moment at the Spring Fling image, while Carly asked Maggie more questions.

Anita touched his arm. "Are you all right?"

He snapped his gaze up as if being pulled out of a fog. "Yeah . . . it's just surreal, I guess. Gramps isn't making things up. It's complicated too. I mean, I thought my grandmother was the love of his life."

"Maybe she was," Anita said. "Most of us have relationships before settling on our true love." Her face felt hot. "Or . . . sometimes the first love doesn't work out."

Wyatt gazed at her for a moment. "Yeah, you're right. Just because Gramps cared about Susan doesn't mean he didn't love my grandma."

By the time the pages had finished printing, Maggie's

group was ready to be transported back to the senior center, where they'd share a meal together. "It was wonderful meeting all of you," she said. "I hope to see you again sometime."

Anita rose to walk her out of the room. "How often do you come here?"

"The excursion is every Monday, but I come maybe once or twice a month." Maggie grasped her hand. "Lovely to meet you and your daughter. Wyatt is a nice man too."

"Wonderful to meet you as well."

Maggie smiled and patted Anita's arm, then she moved away, joining the senior group.

She had a strange feeling as Maggie walked away as if she'd just said goodbye to an old friend. But that was impossible—they'd only met an hour ago.

Eleven

SAM WASN'T EXPECTING A PHONE call on a Monday evening so late. When Wyatt called him, it was usually right after the dinner hour, but now it was eight p.m. Who could be ringing him now? He knew it wasn't Paula. She either called in the morning on one of her shift breaks or not at all. And really, there was no one else in his life who'd call. Sure, he had a visit once in a while from Charles Benson, his longtime neighbor. But Sam happened to know the man was on a vacation with his kids and grandkids.

"Hello? Who's this?" he said into the receiver after picking it up. Might as well get to the point.

"Gramps?"

"Wyatt," he said, relief running through him.

"I wondered if it's too late to come over tonight. I found some yearbook pages you might be interested in seeing."

"*Yearbook*, did you say?" Sam set a bookmark in the book he'd been reading. "I haven't seen any yearbooks around for years."

"I found this at the library," Wyatt said. "Well, we did. I'm with Anita and Carly."

Sam wasn't sure he was catching on to what Wyatt was trying to tell him. "Why are you with them at the library?"

"I can explain everything when we get there."

Sam glanced at the clock on the wall just above the

bookcase. He was usually in bed with his book by nine o'clock as opposed to in his chair with his book right before that. His eyes were already tired, and Wyatt sounded like he had more hours in him.

"How about tomorrow after dinner?" he said. "I'm not going anywhere."

There was a pause and some hushed conversation on the other end of the line.

"Wyatt?"

"Oh yes, sorry. That will be fine. We'll see you tomorrow at six thirty."

After hanging up with Wyatt, Sam picked up his book again, but his mind wouldn't focus on the words. He should have asked his grandson which yearbook he'd found. Was it the one that had Susan in the pictures, or was it the following year, when her missing presence was like a black hole in his heart?

A few more moments passed as he let his memories return. The Spring Fling dance had been their one and only date. Sure, they'd spent time together every chance they had, but after the dance, life had become a whirlwind of Susan's family preparing to move. Sam had volunteered to help them pack their things and set up what they wanted to leave behind at a rummage sale. He remembered feeling like although Susan hadn't left yet, he already missed her. He didn't know at the time that he'd never see her again, that their letters would be the only connection that would remain after their childhood spent together.

Sam rose from his chair and went through his bedtime routine. If he took things slowly, he could do everything on his own. He wasn't at the point where one of the aides had to help him change his clothing or wash up. Climbing into bed, he left his book on the nightstand, still bookmarked.

He didn't need to read to fall asleep tonight. He had plenty of memories to sort through. But mostly he wondered how Susan was doing after all these years. If her marriage had been happy. If her children were well. And did she have grandchildren?

"Mr. Davis? Time for your morning medications."

Sam opened his eyes, surprised to see that his room glowed with morning sunlight. He'd slept through the entire night without waking up once.

Ginny smiled down at him. "Sleep well?"

"I . . ." He cleared his throat. "I slept like the dead. What time is it and where am I?"

Thankfully, Ginny was used to his quips. She laughed and held out a glass of water and a small paper cup of pills. He moved to one elbow and took the pills, then swallowed down some water.

While he remained in bed for a few more minutes, Ginny bustled about the room. She emptied the garbage, folded the throw on his recliner, straightened a few books on the bookshelf.

Once Sam felt awake enough to get out of bed, he pushed back the covers, then swung his legs over the edge.

"How are you feeling?" Ginny asked.

"Fine." And he did feel fine. Well-rested. No headache. No vertigo. The only thing he noticed was his stomach rumbling. "Hungry."

She smiled. "We can head to breakfast as soon as you're ready."

Sam knew if he'd complained about anything, then Ginny would have offered to bring his breakfast on a tray. But she was also of the mind that if he had the physical strength, then he should have breakfast in the dining room. "You need to stay social," she'd told him more than once.

The Healing Garden

She brought over the walker, and although Sam didn't like to use it in his bedroom, previous incidents had shown him that his legs and balance were not always reliable first thing in the morning.

He grasped the handle and pushed to his feet. So far, so good. "My grandson is visiting tonight after dinner," he said, "so I'll be staying in the dining room for that."

"I'll leave a message for tonight's staff," Ginny said.

Sam nodded and headed into the bathroom. He shut the door, but didn't lock it. In fact, the door didn't lock in case there was some sort of emergency. He washed up, then spent a moment studying his face in the mirror. He'd have to ask for a shave today, though his whiskers didn't grow as fast as they used to. He only made the request a couple times a week.

A memory flashed through his mind of when Susan first noticed he was growing stubble. She'd teased him about it and then asked to feel his jaw.

Memories were strange things. Sometimes they were murky, like a hazy day. Other times they felt like the event only happened a few days ago. Right now, Sam could remember details of that moment when Susan ran her fingers over his jaw. The way her eyes had crinkled at the corners. How she wore a smirk he was so familiar with. The strawberry scent of her shampoo as she leaned close. The sensation of a girl—a pretty girl who was his best friend—touching him. How she'd drawn back and laughed, then said coyly, "My friend is turning into a man."

Was that when Sam had fallen in love with her? Or was it much sooner? Maybe that was when he finally had hope that she'd view him as someone other than her lanky best friend. He'd been all elbows and knees for years, until the summer between their sophomore and junior years. His family had gone on a road trip vacation for eight days, and when they returned, it was to a much more mature-looking Susan. And he supposed he'd changed, too, in that short time. Or maybe it had seemed that way since they'd never been apart for long. Until she'd moved for good.

"Mr. Davis? Need help with anything?" Ginny's voice tugged him out of his revelry.

"No, I'm coming right out." He rinsed out the sink, dried his hands, then opened the door.

By the time he was in the dining room and seated next to a few other residents for breakfast, he was back to reality. Back to the routine. Back to scrambled eggs and a piece of toast with grape jelly. He didn't pay much attention to the announcement about the activities going on that day. He might or might not join in. His gaze cut to the large bank of windows that framed the makings of a mild, sunny day. A break in the clouds was always welcome. Beyond the windows grew a walled-in garden that contained a circular walking path and a few benches nestled among the flower beds. A nice change in atmosphere.

He took a final sip of his orange juice, then excused himself from the buzzing conversation at his table that he hadn't been paying attention to anyway. Using his walker so he didn't potentially get stuck somewhere if he got a hitch in his knee or hip, he headed toward the walled garden.

"Mr. Davis, where are you going?" He looked over to see Ginny walking toward him.

"I'm going to walk the garden path for a while," he said. "No need to follow."

Ginny paused in her step and smiled. "All right, sir. Let me know if you change your mind. I'll be close by."

She would indeed, but Sam didn't need the extra assistance today. His legs felt steady, and it might have

The Healing Garden

something to do with wanting to have a good day so by the time Wyatt came, he'd be ready to walk down memory lane. Entering the garden, he turned right on the path. The scents of roses and other flowering plants immediately surrounded him.

"There he is," a woman's voice said, "the lone bachelor."

Sam could guess the voice belonged to Kathy or Debbie—two women who were always up to something. They lived across the hall from each other in the women's section. When he'd first come to the center, he'd been seated at their table, so he'd gotten an earful of their lives at each meal. They weren't related, but somehow they looked like sisters. Both with silver-gray hair cut short, dark arched eyebrows, and a habit of wearing ruby-red lipstick. He only knew the exact color because they had told him, then proceeded to put it on right after their meals were eaten.

"I think he's ignoring us," the other woman's voice said.

A couple of steps later, and they came into view. Today they were wearing matching cardigans and sitting on a bench. One of them—Kathy—held a book, and Debbie held a small bag of potato chips. How she managed to end up with extra snacks was a mystery to him.

"I'm not ignoring anyone," Sam said. "I'm simply taking a walk."

Both women smiled innocently at him as if they hadn't just been giving him guff.

"That's wonderful, Sam," Kathy gushed.

"You're looking healthy today," Debbie added.

It was assisted living lingo, he guessed, to "look healthy" even though they were all here in this place together as their final destination in life.

"Do you want to sit with us?" Kathy asked, her lipsticked smile bright. "We're having a book club meeting."

Sam slowed in his step and came to a stop. "Book club with two people?"

Debbie lifted her chin. "You can have a book club with only one person, you know. And if you join us, we'll have three."

Sam had to chuckle even if he wasn't sure if Debbie was trying to be funny. "I haven't read the book."

This prompted Kathy to hold up hers. "No need to read in advance. We won't give away the ending."

"We never give away the ending," Debbie said. "Besides, we usually can't remember it. Does that happen to you? We know you're a big reader."

"It depends on how long ago I read the book." He pushed the walker forward again to continue his walk. "Enjoy your book club."

"We will," Kathy said. "And if you want to join us next week, we're reading *Little Women*."

"And . . ." Debbie rattled her chip bag. "There will be snacks."

Sam chuckled and continued walking. He was past them now, but that didn't stop Kathy from calling out, "We always have snacks, you can be assured of that."

Sharing a small bag of chips wasn't all that tempting to him. Besides, he didn't have a copy of *Little Women*, although he knew he'd read it at some point. One of his years in high school? About the only thing he remembered was that one of the characters was a writer and her sister died. Sad stuff. Maybe if he could drum up a copy, he'd read it since he didn't have much else on his agenda for the week.

He walked slowly on purpose so he could breathe in the earthy scents mixed with the fragrance of blooming flowers. It reminded him of Norma, when she had to quit her full-time job because of her heart condition. She'd wanted to stay busy, just on a more restful scale. Although some days that she spent in the garden, he worried she'd overtax herself.

Boy, he missed her. They hadn't been in love when they'd married. No, the circumstances were a bit unusual, but looking back, he didn't regret anything. Susan had been out of his life for years, and he was available to help Norma. His heart would follow later.

Once Sam made it back to his room, a copy of *Little Women* in hand that he'd found at the center's library, he settled into his recliner, intent on reading until lunchtime. He got caught up in the story well enough, smiling because Jo's personality reminded him of Susan—giving and industrious. Not afraid to speak her mind. But as his eyes grew heavy and he slipped into a nap, it wasn't Susan who was on his mind, but Norma.

She'd been the girlfriend of David Gerber, who Sam had crossed paths with a couple of times when a large group of them went bowling on Saturday nights. Norma was tall, willowy, and bookish. They got into more than one conversation about books, and Sam had never considered it flirting, but apparently David did.

They'd had a confrontation one night after the bowling alley that almost came to fisticuffs. David had shoved Sam, and he shoved the guy back. They were evenly matched, but a crowd had gathered, and Norma had tearfully pleaded for David to back down. It seemed he'd been in trouble with the cops for something else, and she didn't want new charges brought against him.

It was the last time he saw Norma or David for a few months. They hadn't disappeared exactly, but they stopped coming to bowling night. Then one evening, after Sam had finished working the late shift, he'd stopped by the diner on the corner just on the edge of his neighborhood. He knew the kitchen of his college apartment probably only had a box of crackers, and he was starving.

He ordered enough for three people and sat down to wait while Hal prepared his order. That's when he noticed the far table in the corner, where a young woman was sipping a drink, tears streaking her cheeks. His heart went out to her, but he aimed to mind his own business and leave her to her own troubles, when he realized it was Norma.

She looked up and recognized him too. They ended up spending the next two hours talking and eating—Sam had plenty of food to share. She was still dating that doofus David, but Sam remembered coming away from talking to her thinking how her boyfriend didn't know how lucky he was. Norma was a great gal with a bright future. She was acing her classes in clerical school and planned to work for either a hospital or law firm when she graduated.

David had no such aspirations and was working as a part-time mechanic. It was honest labor, though, and nothing that Sam could criticize. Only his personality needed some work. Apparently he hated reading and thought it was a waste of time for Norma. Which was why she brought a book with her to the diner while David hung out with his buddies on card night.

Over the next few weeks, Sam would randomly run into Norma at the diner. They'd share a table and food, which he insisted on paying for. He ordered extra if he saw her sitting in the corner booth when he arrived. She always had a book with her, but she bookmarked it as soon as he came over to her table. Sam supposed he should have felt a twinge of guilt spending so much time with another man's girl, but there was nothing romantic between them.

She was pretty and sweet, sure, but he knew from the get-go that she was taken.

Until she wasn't.

A tap on the door pulled him from his circling dreams about Norma. He drew in a sharp breath. It was the second time that day that someone had awakened him from sleep.

"Come in," he called in a rasp. "I'm presentable."

The door opened, and Ginny walked in. It took her only seconds to assess the situation. "Having a nap?"

"Something like that." He stifled a yawn. "What's this? Blood pressure time?"

"Yes, I'm afraid so." She didn't look apologetic, though. All smiles, she bent to strap on the blood pressure cuff. In moments, she was finished. "Everything looks good. You ready for lunch?"

"I suppose," he said.

Ginny smiled and adjusted the walker so it would be easier for him to grip and stand. Her gaze didn't miss much because she said, "You switched books, huh? *Little Women* is a classic."

"I'm in a book club."

Ginny didn't even look surprised. "I see Kathy and Debbie snagged you."

"That's right. I hope I know what I'm getting into." Sam nodded toward the book on the side table. "How much trouble can there be with discussing *Little Women*?"

"With Kathy and Debbie as part of the discussion?" Ginny chuckled. "Just make sure you're a huge fan of Louisa May Alcott or there'll be trouble."

He shuffled toward the door. "I'll be ready for it."

The afternoon passed quickly, which pleased him, because he was looking forward to Wyatt's visit. Sam wasn't expecting him to bring Anita and Carly, though, so it was a nice surprise when the three of them showed up.

"Well, I wasn't expecting a whole crew," he said, smiling

as they approached the table where he waited. Then he remembered. "Your car was having trouble, right?"

"Right," Anita said. "It's in the shop. Needs a new starter."

Sam didn't miss the crease of her brow. Car trouble was never a pleasant thing, but he was happy to see them, nonetheless.

"We got a ride with Wyatt," Carly said. "Mostly because we wouldn't let him come without us."

"Oh?" Sam wondered at the excitement in her eyes. He wanted to ask her about school and how her quest for new friends was going, but Wyatt had already settled on one side of him.

"Here, Gramps," he said softly. "We brought you some copies of your yearbook, and we'd love to talk to you about some of the photos. Anita and Carly went to the library with me to look through the old yearbooks."

"Ah, that was kind of everyone . . ." Sam glanced at his inquisitive audience, wondering what exactly was going on.

"It wouldn't have happened without Anita's prodding," Wyatt said. "I was reluctant, but she insisted."

"Not exactly *insisted*," she countered with a coy smile.

Wyatt smiled at her in return, and her cheeks were pinker than Sam remembered. She sat on the other side of Carly, her eyes focused on Wyatt more than anyone else at their table.

Sam didn't miss the studied glance that Wyatt gave Anita, the curve of a quick smile, before he opened the folder he'd brought.

Sam dropped his gaze before he let his mind draw conclusions where there might not be any. Maybe Wyatt and Anita were just friends, but he couldn't remember a time when he'd seen Wyatt's attention so captured by another woman. He hadn't brought anyone home to meet him for years.

Wyatt tapped the first page. "These aren't the best copies since they came from a microfiche machine."

Sam began to leaf through the pages. He didn't speak for a moment, because he knew exactly what the photos were and the year and month they were all taken. It wasn't something that he could forget.

"That's me and Susan," he said, tapping on a photo. "Our first and last date, you could say." He raised his gaze to meet his grandson's. "She was a remarkable person."

Wyatt nodded. "She's the one who sent that postcard a few months ago?"

"You believe me now." Sam hadn't expected the flush of guilt across Wyatt's face.

"I . . . I do believe you," he said. "I'm sorry I didn't before."

It was a fair apology. "Thought my mind was going?"

When Wyatt's face paled, Sam chuckled. "Don't worry, I know I'm getting on in years. Some things will eventually go. My memories can be foggy, but not about Susan. She was my best friend, you know."

Wyatt swallowed. "I know. You've said that, but since you only recently brought her up, I had wondered if your memories were true. I'm sorry for doubting you."

"I understand. You were thinking of your grandmother . . . and wanting to protect her memory." Sam turned the next page to where Susan posed with her glee club. He used to go to the practices when he had time, just to hear her sing. If he'd been able to carry a tune, he would have joined. He lifted his gaze, not realizing he'd spoken his thoughts aloud.

Everyone was watching him. "Susan was my soulmate, I

think. Is that what they call it nowadays? When her family moved, I never doubted that I'd see her again. We'd have much more freedom as adults, I assumed. But life happened, and the years passed. I met Norma, and Susan had moved on with another fella—at least that's what her letters seemed to indicate."

He tapped a finger against the glee club photo. "Susan got engaged, and I moved on with my life too. We stopped writing letters, and I wasn't even sure if she was still in Nevada. I only wished the best for her, of course." His voice trailed off.

"So you never heard from her again until the postcard?" Carly asked eagerly.

"That's right." Sam looked up from the black-and-white photo of a smiling Susan. "I was shocked to receive it. But I knew immediately that it was from the right Susan. I don't know her circumstances right now. She might have a dozen grandchildren and a busy life. Maybe she sent the postcard hoping it might reach me. Or perhaps she knew I still lived in the same home I'd grown up in?"

Wyatt patted his arm. "We're happy to hear any stories you want to tell us, Gramps."

Sam drew in a breath. "I suppose the older I get, the shorter my life seems, and my high school years don't seem all that long ago. I mean, I know that decades have passed, but I'd like to catch up with Susan. Find out which path her life took."

Wyatt's shoulders slumped, but he said in an upbeat voice, "Maybe we can track down her address and you can write to her?"

Sam clasped his hands atop his table. "Finding her address would be important," he said. "Because I'd like to visit her in person, while I still can."

Wyatt frowned, as Sam suspected he might. "If you

can't take me, then maybe your sister can."

"We don't even know where she lives," Wyatt said. "Or if she'd welcome a visit."

"We'll find her phone number, then." Sam settled his gaze on Anita. "Maybe you can help if Wyatt's too busy?"

Twelve

ANITA BLINKED, NOT SURE IF she understood Mr. Davis's request to track down a phone number for Susan. Surely Wyatt could do that. Then she realized . . . Mr. Davis was trying to get her to support his goal to contact Susan.

Wyatt had been the one to agree to find the yearbook in the first place, and Anita didn't want to get in the middle of any family debate.

Wyatt's gaze was on her, and he wasn't jumping in to answer, so she said, "I'm happy to help with whatever is agreed upon." There. That was neutral, right?

"I can help too," Carly said. "Our school librarian had us learn about censuses before."

Everyone looked over at Carly, and Mr. Davis said, "That's an excellent idea."

"Gramps . . ." Wyatt said in a soft, questioning tone.

"Carly, why don't you go ask one of the aides if we could get some drinks at our table?" Anita suggested.

She popped to her feet. "Okay."

With her daughter gone for a few minutes, Anita turned to the men. "Carly and I can give you some privacy. I'm truly happy to help with anything, but I don't want to be in the middle."

"You're not in the middle," Wyatt said at the same time that Mr. Davis said, "You can be in the middle if it means finding Susan."

The Healing Garden

Wyatt's expression went still, and Anita wished she could backtrack. Maybe by not coming to the center tonight with him. Mr. Davis wasn't her grandfather, and she knew Wyatt was trying to be supportive despite his complicated feelings. But tracking down the truth about Susan was a lot different than tracking her down in person.

"Gramps, I need to talk to Anita for a second," Wyatt said just as Carly came back, balancing four cups of water.

"Thanks, Carly," she said, smiling. "Wait here with Mr. Davis. Wyatt and I will be right back."

Mr. Davis didn't seem to mind, and he and Carly fell into conversation about her school. Anita followed Wyatt out to the lobby.

He moved to one of the large windows that framed the orange sky from the setting sun. A line had appeared between his brows. Shoving his hands into his pockets, he said, "I didn't expect Gramps to want to track her down. I don't know if that's the best idea . . ."

Anita had been surprised as well, but maybe not as surprised as him. "Maybe a phone call with her will answer any of his questions, and maybe it will bring them both some peace."

Wyatt looked down at the ground. "Maybe." He sighed, then met her gaze. "Was he in love with Susan? I mean, he hasn't denied it—and they were dating—but was he in love with her the whole time he was married to my grandmother? Or is he just distracting himself from truly grieving over my grandmother?"

"I think he was devoted to your grandma," Anita said quietly. She wasn't sure where the assurance was coming from, but she didn't see Mr. Davis as someone who didn't care about his wife. He served in the war. He had to be a realist. A man who could care deeply too. "Maybe now that he's a widower, he's curious about people in his past."

"You're right," Wyatt conceded. "But curiosity is one thing. Following through—and reaching out—is another thing."

Anita nodded and fell silent. The orange of the sunset began to fade to a burnished red. "Maybe this can be taken one step at a time. You don't even know if she can be tracked down. Phone books, censuses, calling a city records office . . . all of it might be a dead end."

Wyatt rubbed the back of his neck. "I worry that he hasn't dealt with his grief over Grandma. That he'll spend his energy on this Susan woman, only to be crushed again. For whatever reason."

"We can't predict any of that." Anita took a couple steps closer to the window, and Wyatt joined her. Together they watched as the brilliant colors of the sunset faded.

"We should get back," he said after a moment. "Before my grandpa talks your daughter into some sort of escapade."

Anita smiled and looked over at him. "They're often in cahoots about something."

"She's been good for him," Wyatt said, sincerity in his tone as his gaze held hers. "The past couple of weeks, he's been more cheerful, more alive. As if he's looking forward to each day."

Anita swallowed back the emotion. "He's been good for her too. It was a stressful weekend when we came for that first visit. I was sure I'd be taking home a grumpy teenager to deal with on my own. But only a short time with your grandfather, and Carly gained a new perspective on some things."

Wyatt's gaze hadn't left her face, and she loved that he was really listening to her. He'd loosened his tie at his throat, and scrubbed his hand through his hair more than once, giving it a rumpled look. Put-together Wyatt was a nice visual, but Wyatt a bit on the edge was also appealing.

She pushed those thoughts away. "What do you want to do? I don't want to step on anyone's toes."

"Gramps is set on this," he said. "That look in his eye has never changed. Even as a kid, I knew it meant he wouldn't be changing his mind." He set his hands on his hips. "I just wish I knew if this is going to be a fruitless search."

"None of us can know what's on the other end of this search," she said. "Maybe whatever this is will bring him some peace about his past."

Wyatt frowned at that. "What do you mean?"

"He seems to be sharing nostalgic memories, but I think some of them have a double meaning. I think he's looking for closure on something that happened between him and Susan."

His brows lifted. "You're either very observant or very wrong."

Anita didn't mind being called out. She could be wrong, but they'd never know until Wyatt followed this trail his grandpa wanted to take.

"All right," he said suddenly. "I'll find Susan for my grandpa. Do you think you could help? I mean . . . at least be my sounding board if you don't have time to do any sleuthing."

He sounded so frazzled that Anita didn't know whether to comfort him or laugh. She set a hand on his arm. "I can help."

His shoulders visibly relaxed, and his gaze moved to where she touched him. "Okay, thank you," he said quietly. "That means a lot."

Anita dropped her hand. "No problem. I think Carly and I are pretty invested now."

The edge of his mouth lifted, and she loved seeing the worry lines ease. From her outsider's point of view, this all sounded like an interesting quest. But from Wyatt's point of view, she could see how it would tangle up his emotions.

"He's probably talking Carly's ear off right now," Wyatt said. "Let's go back in and give him the news."

"Sounds good." She turned toward the hallway leading to the dining room, and his hand touched the small of her back. For only an instant. Then his touch was gone. She shouldn't be feeling the warmth spread through her, but she was.

Back inside the dining room, Carly and Mr. Davis were playing a game of Uno. A change of pace from their usual Scrabble, but no less competitive. He set down his cards the moment he spotted them. "Well? Conference over? What did you decide?"

Wyatt sat on the other side of his grandpa, and Anita took her usual place by Carly.

"We're going to track down Susan," Wyatt said. "All of us."

"Me too?" Carly asked, her eyes bright.

"You too," Anita said with a smile.

Mr. Davis sat back in his chair, a triumphant grin on his face. "Excellent. When do we start?"

Wyatt chuckled. "I can start making calls tomorrow. But first, we need to know as many names and dates as you can remember. There might be more than one Susan Martin out there."

"Should we start with Medford?" Carly asked.

Mr. Davis smiled. "You remembered the postmark."

She nodded. "Maybe we should just fly to Medford and start knocking on doors that belong to all the Susan Martins."

He chuckled. "There's a few problems with that. First, I don't fly, and second, I don't know what her married name is."

Everyone at the table went silent. "I didn't think of that," Wyatt finally said, rubbing his forehead. "That should have been our first consideration."

"It's only a minor bump," Mr. Davis said. "We'll just have to find out when she married so we can find out who she married."

Anita didn't know what was going through Wyatt's mind, but everything just got a lot more complicated. Instead of this project maybe taking a few nights of phone calls, this could stretch into weeks of phone calls, writing letters, and requesting records they may or may not be given access to.

"Got something to write on?" Mr. Davis asked his grandson. "I'll give you the names of her family members. Although her mother died about a year after they moved."

Wyatt was empty-handed, so Anita pulled out a small notebook from her purse that she used to jot down her grocery list. "I've got something."

Mr. Davis rattled off the names of Susan's parents and siblings, as well as the name of the uncle they went to live with when they first moved.

Then he picked up his Uno cards. "I'll let the two of you percolate over the details while I beat Carly in Uno."

"Hey," Carly said. "You're putting your cart before the horse."

Anita chuckled. "I haven't heard that saying in years, probably decades."

Carly shrugged, and Mr. Davis only smiled. In moments, they were enmeshed in their game. Wyatt rose and moved to sit next to Anita. "Well? Any idea of where to start?"

She turned the notebook toward him so he could see all the names. "We should probably start with the uncle's name. Find out the name of the company he owned in Nevada. Then see if we can get a list of former employees?"

"Good idea." Wyatt tapped the paper with the names. "We could call the city hall of the town and find out if we can access any marriage records."

"Okay, I like it." She paused.

He looked at her expectantly. "Do you want to get together tomorrow afternoon? Join forces with our phone calls?"

"What time can you get off?" she asked. "Most businesses will close by five. At least Nevada is in the same time zone as we are."

"I'll go into work extra early so I can leave close to three. Then I'll head over to your place, unless you and Carly want to come to mine?"

"My place will be faster," Anita said. "I won't have to wait for Carly to get home from school."

Just the thought of Wyatt walking into her house had her thinking of all the things she should probably straighten up or clean. Not that she intended to deep clean or anything, but she wanted things more decent than what they were.

"All right," he said in a low voice. "I'll plan on being to your place no later than three thirty tomorrow. If anything changes, I'll give you a call."

Anita bit her lip and nodded. It was a plan. Her week was definitely turning out to be much different than she could have predicted.

Thirteen

1922

SAM GOT OFF WORK A few minutes earlier than usual, and it only put an extra spring in his step as he headed to the café for something to eat. He wasn't fooling himself that he hoped Norma would be there. They'd become good friends, he surmised. He'd told her about Susan, and she told him a little about David.

A couple of weeks earlier, he'd received a letter from Susan saying that she was engaged to her fellow. Sam knew she'd been going steady with a guy for a few months. But he was taken aback when her letter came. It seemed that things had moved very fast between them . . . And now they were going to get married?

He'd shown up at the café carrying a whirlwind of emotions. Norma had let him blow off his steam, and when he'd calmed, she helped him see that the Susan of today was probably not the Susan of high school. Years had passed, and although they'd kept up their letter writing, neither of them had made the huge effort to travel across several states to see each other.

"That's because every time I make a plan, something happens to derail it," Sam had defended. Then he'd gone quiet. He'd let the canceled plans put him into a funk until he came up with another way to visit Susan. A few times she'd had hopes that she might be able to return to Seattle too, but money always stood in her way. Even when Sam had offered to send her a ticket, she'd told him to keep it for tuition. Which he really did need to pay, but had continuing his crush on Susan been unrealistic?

Talking to Norma had helped him see things in a different way. So when news of Susan's engagement came, she was the one he confided in. Because it meant that any hope he'd had as a teenager of spending the rest of his life with Susan had died once and for all.

Tonight though, he had good news to share with her. He'd passed his check ride for a monoplane, which meant he'd be starting the next phase of the aviation program. He entered the café to find Norma at her usual table. She had a drink in front of her, absently stirring it with a straw, but her expression told him she was upset about something. So instead of ordering right away, he headed toward the table in the corner.

She glanced up at him as he slid into the booth across from her, then lowered her eyes again.

"Hey," he said gently.

"Hey," she whispered.

He waited a moment, but when she didn't say anything more, he continued. "What's wrong, Norma?"

She blinked and tears fell on her cheeks, then her face crumpled.

Sam rose from his spot and sat on her bench. "What's going on?" he asked, setting his arm about her shoulders.

She leaned against him, her shoulders shaking with her mostly silent crying. "I . . . it's . . ."

"David?" he guessed.

She nodded against his chest.

The Healing Garden

"Did he break up with you?"

Another nod.

"He's a piece of work," Sam said on an angry exhale. "Don't give him a second thought. You can do way better than the likes of him."

Norma wrapped her arms about his torso, and he tightened his hold on her. He'd never touched her before, never hugged her, but this felt nice—comforting. She smelled faintly of roses—maybe it was her shampoo or perfume she'd put on that morning.

"Seriously, Norma," he said, rubbing her arm. "You get one night to cry over him, but after tonight, no more. Do I need to cut him off at the knees?"

"No," she said with a soft laugh.

Laughing was much better than crying, Sam decided.

"He's gone." Her voice was muffled by his shirt.

"What do you mean, gone?"

"He took off to California. Going to work at his cousin's auto shop."

"He works at the auto shop here," Sam said with a frown. "Didn't invite you? Or you didn't want to go?"

Norma finally lifted her head and drew away from him. He handed over a napkin and she mopped her face. Even though her eyes were reddened, they were still a pretty brown. Her cheeks had flushed a deep pink, matching the color of her lovely lips. Sam blinked, pushing those thoughts away. This was a woman in mourning, and he didn't need to be thinking about how pretty and kissable she looked.

"I don't know anything anymore," Norma said in a pained voice. "Last night I found out some news, and when I told him, he put together a plan to get away from me."

None of this made any sense. David had been so possessive of her, and she seemed content enough with him. So why the change of heart? "What was the news?"

She looked down at her twisting hands. "I'm pregnant."

Sam felt as if all the air had been sucked from his lungs. It took him a moment to understand the enormity of what she was saying. "And David doesn't want the baby?"

"No," she whispered. "He told me it wasn't his, and that I better not come after him for any money or support." The tears were back, and her voice trembled at the next words. "He called me awful things. All lies. I've never been with anyone . . . except him." She used the napkin again.

Sam didn't know what to say. This was a tangle, that was for sure. Maybe David was in shock? Maybe he'd come around? Not that he wanted Norma to forgive the jerk, but wasn't it better for a kid to have a dad around?

"I'm sorry." He grasped her hand and held on. What else could he say? "What do your parents think?"

She gave a half-laugh that had no joy in it. "They want me to move to Portland to stay with my aunt until the baby is born, then place it for adoption."

It sounded gut-wrenching to Sam. "What do *you* want?"

Norma threw up her hands. "It's all so new, all so much . . . I don't know what I want. I thought that David would—" She covered her mouth with her hand and closed her eyes.

"Want to marry you," Sam finished.

She nodded, the pain etching lines about her eyes. "I want the baby, I do. Even with David's rejection, I still can't imagine giving my baby up. But I don't have a choice." She folded her arms against her chest. "It's not fair for me to bring this child into the world with only one parent—and a parent who'd have to be dependent on her own parents."

These things happened sometimes. It could all work out, although right now it felt heavy.

"You have nine months to decide, right?" Sam said,

hoping to ease the situation. "You don't have to decide everything right now. Everyone is reeling and making rush judgments."

"More like seven months," Norma said. "Besides, my parents already bought me a train ticket for Friday."

Friday was two days away.

"My aunt is preparing a room for me," she continued. "I'm not going to be called her niece when I'm there. I'll be a friend's daughter." Her eyes watered again. "I'm a shame to everyone, yet David gets to start a new carefree life."

It wasn't fair, none of it was fair. Norma was paying all the consequences of a two-partner relationship. "Maybe your parents will change their minds."

She didn't look hopeful, though. "My mother's been shut in her room all day, and my father stayed home from work to make all the arrangements. They're not going to change their minds."

Sam gazed at the tabletop, his eyes following the path of a couple scratches in the scrubbed wood. "I'll track down David and talk to him. He needs to take responsibility."

She set her hand on his arm. "No. I . . . the last month things have been off between us. He was calling me moody—and maybe I was. At least I know I had an excuse. But I caught him lying to me more than once about his whereabouts."

He furrowed his brows, looking at the hand on his arm, then meeting her gaze.

She drew in a breath. "I think he was stepping out on me. In fact, I know it. Not that he confessed, but my gut is telling me not to ignore the warning signs."

Hot anger raced through him, and his jaw tensed. "I'm tracking him down anyway. He needs to be taught a lesson."

"Sam," she said, her voice pleading. "He's already left

for California. I guess he didn't want my father banging down his door. Besides, I'm finished with him. You were right all along."

For once, he didn't want to be right. Not about this. Or at least not with Norma ending up pregnant and alone. He wanted to be right two months ago and have her dump the idiot. "He shouldn't be able to get away with this," Sam ground out. "I'll track him down in California and—"

"No," Norma said, her voice stronger now. "You're my best friend, Sam. I need you here, with me. I need you to be my friend for the next two days before I'm shipped off to my aunt's. Then I need you to continue with your own life. Live your dreams for me while I'm gone. And then maybe, someday, when I'm back, we can have our late-night talks at this café again. It will give me something to look forward to."

She was crying again, and Sam rubbed at his jaw, his own tears starting.

With Norma going away, he'd be losing his best friend too. Again. How had it all come to this?

"Now, listen to me," she said with a steadying breath. "I'm starving. Can you order some food? I don't want to waste our last couple of days together with sad stuff. Let's eat and talk about you for a change."

Sam decided that Norma was the strongest woman he knew. He moved out of the booth, put in a giant order of food, then did just as she asked. They talked for the next couple of hours about his schooling, his flight training, what she'd pack for Oregon, how she hoped to take a leave of absence from clerical school and return in eight months.

By the end of the night, a plan had formed in his mind. He left Norma's side with a hug and a kiss on the cheek. Walking home in the opposite direction of her place, he slipped his hands into his pockets, hunching his shoulders forward. They were meeting again tomorrow night at the café. And before that happened, he had several things to do.

The following morning, Sam made his inquiries, then he visited Norma's father. The man was surprised to hear about his plan, but he didn't protest. Sam considered that a sign he was doing the right thing. Now, all he had to do was convince Norma.

The day passed quickly, and when night fell, he headed to the café. But Norma wasn't there. Sam told himself not to panic. He was earlier than usual since he'd taken most of the day off to get his errands done. His stomach was too knotted up to eat any of the food that he'd ordered in good faith, hoping Norma would indeed be showing up.

As the minutes ticked by, he began to imagine all sorts of scenarios. Her father had changed his mind, or Norma had fallen ill with her pregnancy, or David had turned back around and swept her off her feet . . .

"Sam?"

He snapped his head up. There stood Norma, her brow puckered in concern.

"I wondered if you'd fallen asleep sitting up," she said with a smile—a smile that struck him in the chest. How had he not noticed how pretty and sweet she was? Well, he'd noticed, but he'd never internalized it before.

"No." Sam pushed to his feet. "I was, uh, thinking."

Her brows lifted, and she slid into the booth seat across from him. "You were waiting for me?"

A spread of untouched food sat on the table. He'd barely sipped his drink. And the drink he'd bought for her had its ice mostly melted.

"Yeah, are you hungry?" Suddenly he didn't know what to say, or how to begin.

"Definitely hungry." She took a long sip of the Coca-Cola, then stabbed a fork into the garden salad.

Sam reached for his drink as well and gulped half of it down.

Her forehead creased. "Something's off about you. What's going on? Are you sick?"

"No." He pushed the drink aside. "I'm not sick. I'm . . . I need to talk to you, Norma, and I want you to know that I'm in earnest. And you need to know this has nothing to do with Susan being engaged." Or at least he didn't think it did. He'd decided not to let that thought go deeper. "I visited your father this afternoon."

"What? Why?" Her eyes widened. "Did you try to talk him out of sending me to Portland? He was probably furious."

"Not exactly," Sam said. "I mean, I did talk him out of sending you to Portland, but it's not what you think."

Her mouth opened, then shut.

Sam reached for her hand. "Norma, I'm sorry for all that's been happening in your life. You must know that you're my best friend too, and the best part of my week is sitting with you at this café. You make me laugh. You encourage me. You give me hope for a good future. You're a bright, talented woman, and you're drop-dead beautiful."

Her cheeks went from pink to red.

"I know that you cared for David, and you know that I cared for Susan," he said. "Both of them have moved on, and here we are."

She tilted her head, watching him carefully.

"You're going to be a mother in a few months, and everything's going to change for you," he continued. "I . . . I've been thinking about all of it, considering all the angles, and only one thing makes sense." He drew in a breath. "I don't want to lose you, and I don't want to see you lose something precious to you. So I spoke to your father to get his blessing to ask you to marry me."

Norma stared at him for a second, then she tugged her hand from his and covered her mouth. Tears filled her eyes, and his heart sank. She was angry, hurt, or shocked . . . whatever she was, it wasn't pleased. It wasn't happy or relieved. She didn't love him, and that was okay. He didn't love her in the way that he'd loved Susan. There was potential, though, right? Or at least he thought there was. Yet, Norma had started to cry.

"Look," Sam said, his voice trembling. "I know I'm still in school. I talked to the housing department, and we can get on the waiting list for married housing. It would be small, but it would be ours. Or we could live with your parents if you'd like. It's up to you—whatever you want."

Tears coursed down her cheeks. Would she say something? Had he just decimated their friendship?

"I know I'm not David, and you'll probably never feel for me what you did for him." Sam offered up his last line of reasoning. "But we're compatible and I think that's a good start. Maybe down the road, we'll fall in love with each other. I don't think it would be too hard on my part."

Norma lowered her hand and swiped at her cheeks. "Are you serious, Sam? You'd marry me? I don't need you to feel sorry for me."

"I'd only be sorry if you left for Portland tomorrow," he said, the truth vibrating through him. "If you stayed, then I'd honestly be the luckiest man in Seattle."

She blinked several times, gazing at him, as if waiting for him to laugh and say he was joking about all of it. But he wasn't joking. He'd never been so serious in all his life.

"I don't want you to throw away your future on a mistake I made with another man," she said in a stilted voice.

Sam felt those words right in his gut. The circumstances weren't ideal, that he knew. "We all make mistakes," he said.

"It doesn't mean we have to keep making them. Marry me, Norma. Love me or not. But don't leave me."

He had one more card to play. Sliding off the bench, he knelt on the floor, facing her. Then he pulled out the ring he'd stored in his pocket. It had been his grandmother's ring, and he thought he'd be giving it to Susan one day. It symbolized family, love, devotion, and he wanted Norma to be the woman who wore it. Holding up the ring, he said, "Let's share our future."

Her gaze focused on the ring, then moved to his face. "I don't want to let you down," she whispered.

"You could never let me down," he whispered back.

She leaned forward and took his face in her hands. "I already care about you, Sam Davis. I just didn't want you to regret anything."

He kissed her then. It was a tentative kiss, but it sent his heart galloping. Somewhere in the middle of their kissing, she agreed to marry him. And Sam felt the rightness of her words all the way to his soul.

Fourteen

1981

ANITA SCANNED THE FRONT ROOM that she'd vacuumed and dusted. There wasn't much else to do in preparation for her guest unless she decided to completely redecorate. That wasn't going to happen anytime soon, especially with her car repair bills. The Bug sat beneath the carport now, new starter installed, which had put a sizeable dent in her checkbook.

She'd been distracted most of the day and hadn't made much progress on her newest commissioned art project. She'd had lunch with Phyllis—which was becoming a regular occurrence. Soon after lunch, she gave up on trying to concentrate, and instead baked cookies. Carly would be happy at least. Anita couldn't remember the last time she'd had freshly baked cookies waiting for Carly after school. It was interesting how some traditions faded over time. One day, they were part of regular life, the next, they were a memory.

Anita crossed to the front window and stood where she could see the corner of the street. Wyatt should be arriving in the next few minutes. He hadn't called, so she assumed there hadn't been any work delays. Or Carly could arrive first. She had been walking home with her new friend Sara the past two days, and Anita couldn't be happier for her. Moving on from Samantha and Evie had been a good choice. Not only for Carly's school life, but their home life had been more peaceful.

A cherry-red Cadillac turned onto the street. It had to be Wyatt. She smoothed her hair. She'd brushed it into a low ponytail, not wanting to put too much effort into her appearance. Nerves thrummed through her as it was.

The car slowed and pulled alongside the curb. Anita stepped back, staying out of plain sight as Wyatt climbed out. He wore a button-down shirt, a dark tie, slacks . . . pretty much what she always saw him in. She wondered if he ever dressed down. Well, of course he did, but she was curious all the same.

Her heart rate began to skip as he walked along the sidewalk, then headed up the driveway. She moved into the kitchen, just standing there, waiting for him. She didn't want to open the door mere seconds after he knocked. Anita exhaled, telling herself to calm down. She wasn't a teenager. This wasn't a date. They were two adults working together to help his grandpa. Besides, Carly would be walking in the door soon, and that would keep everyone grounded.

The knock on the door jolted through her. Anita scoffed at herself. There was no reason to be jumpy. She headed into the front room, and after a couple deep breaths, she opened the door.

"Hi," she said.

Wyatt's eyes crinkled at the corners with his smile. "How are you?"

"Fine, fine. Come in. How was work today?"

"I got in extra early, and things wrapped up quickly. So I was happy about that." He glanced about her front room as she led the way to the kitchen.

"That sounds good." The small talk was agonizing.

The Healing Garden

"Well, have a seat. Carly should be here in a moment. I have pens and a notepad and the typewriter. There's the phone and phone book. What else do we need?"

Wyatt moved toward the kitchen table, but he didn't sit down. "Your garden looks amazing."

She followed his gaze to where the back windows overlooked the garden she'd spent years cultivating. "It's a work in progress. Carly used to help me a lot, but now school and homework are a lot busier. So there are places that I've fallen behind on."

Wyatt moved toward the back door. "Can you give me a tour?"

"Um..." Anita had thought they'd start right away making phone calls. They only had a couple of hours before businesses would shut down. But the lighting really was better right now, and she could show him more things. "Sure."

Wyatt had noticed her hesitation. "Or not. I don't want to be nosy."

"It's fine." Anita flashed him a smile, and wished her pulse weren't jumping around so much. Her garden was like a second child. She was proud to show it off, yet it was also very personal. But it wasn't like he was going to criticize anything. "Come on through."

Wyatt stepped out the back door after her, and Sassy showed up, apparently from a reprieve in the garden. "Oh hello," he said. "This your cat?"

"Meow," Sassy answered, rubbing against his legs.

"Sorry about the cat fur," Anita said.

"It's fine." He reached down to give Sassy a scratch. "Friendly cat."

"Yeah, I think she spends more time at the neighbor's than here. You're not allergic?"

"Nope."

Sassy got distracted and bounded off after something. Anita led Wyatt to the worktable.

"This is where you work?" he asked.

"Most of the time," Anita said. "When the weather cooperates, of course." Today, the clouds blocked most of the sun, but the rain had held off.

Wyatt touched the edge of the table. "What's this project?"

"Oh, it's three sisters," she said. The canvas was a large square, and she'd started the dresses on two of the girls, using dark green and deep burgundy leaves for the skirts, and a third one was outlined. "Their mother wants this done before they all become teenagers."

Wyatt studied it for so long that Anita felt antsy.

"You have a remarkable talent," he said at last. "I didn't even know this type of art existed."

She gave a small shrug. "It's all around us. In the trees, the bushes, the flowers. Shapes that resemble people."

He nodded, then his green gaze cut to hers. Out here, in her garden space, her mind started to sort through the leaves and plants she'd choose to create his image. She'd have to mix two greens to get the right shade of his eyes.

"I don't think that stuff has ever crossed my mind." His mouth lifted into a smile. "Like I said, you have a unique talent."

All right then . . . Anita could stare into his eyes longer, or she could get moving to show him around before Carly arrived.

"Mom?" Carly's voice echoed through the house, then a door slammed.

Too late. She was here.

"We're in the garden," Anita called, breaking her gaze from Wyatt's scrutiny.

The Healing Garden

Seconds later, she appeared, backpack slung over her shoulder, face flushed as if she'd run the whole way home from school. And perhaps she had. The cat appeared again and trotted to Carly, who picked it up.

"Oh hi, Mr. Davis," she said.

"Wyatt," he corrected. "How was school?"

"Boring," Carly said, petting the cat. "The only good thing about it was the brownie at lunch."

Anita frowned at her daughter. "Don't tell me you only had a brownie."

She raised her brows in innocence, ignoring the statement. "What are you guys doing? I thought you'd be making a bunch of phone calls."

"Your mom's showing me the garden," Wyatt said. "Wanna come?"

Carly scoffed. "No. Mom will just tell me to weed something."

He chuckled. "It only adds to your life skills."

"I won't have any life skills if I don't eat soon." She looked at Anita. "Can I have that leftover pasta salad from last night?"

It took her a moment to catch up with the conversation. "Uh, yeah, sure."

Carly grinned and headed back inside, carrying the cat.

"I can't believe she only ate a brownie all day," Anita said after she left. "Kids can't focus in class living on sweets."

"Agreed. Does she not pack a lunch?"

Anita had to sigh at that. "She used to, but then it wasn't cool anymore this year. So we've been paying for school lunches—or brownies, I guess."

Wyatt patted her shoulder. "I'm sure it will all balance out in a twenty-four-hour period."

He was right, Anita knew, but she was thinking about

his hand on her shoulder. He moved it and walked past the table to the first row of rosebushes. She'd cultivated various colors, and he bent to touch one of the lavender petals. "I don't think I've seen roses this color before."

"They're hybrid," Anita said, rotating her shoulder. It still felt the same. For the next fifteen minutes, she showed him the various garden quadrants and answered his many questions. He seemed very interested in her answers. She hadn't really talked so in-depth about things like seasonal growing and fertilizer.

"Oh, hello-oo," Phyllis said from her backyard, hovering quite near the fence.

When had she come outside? The woman moved like a cat.

Anita waved at her. "Hi, Phyllis."

"Who's this? Your brother?"

Phyllis very well knew that she didn't have any siblings. "This is a friend of mine, Wyatt Davis. Wyatt, this is my neighbor Phyllis."

"Nice to meet you, Phyllis."

Her eyes narrowed a touch. "Nice to meet you too, Wyatt. Where are you from?"

"Here," he said.

"Oh, that's nice, and what do you do?"

"I'm an accountant."

Phyllis's eyes went wide. "How lovely. Do you do personal taxes?"

"Corporate."

She frowned then. "Very interesting." She paused as if she were about to ask something else, then changed her mind. "Well, nice to meet you, and have a lovely evening, you two."

In seconds, Phyllis was back inside her house.

Wyatt looked over at Anita, his brows raised.

"She's sweet, but quite nosy," Anita said with a shrug. "I've no doubt she's still watching us from one of her windows."

He snapped his gaze back over to the neighbor's house.

"Don't look." She laughed. "Come on, we'll finish the tour."

"Lead the way," he said with a smile.

When they reached the far side of the garden where she grew climbing ivy that sprawled along the cinderblock wall, Wyatt asked, "Did you go to art school? Or is this something you figured out on your own?"

"I went to a semester of art school," Anita said. "Then Bobby and I got married. We'd been together since high school. I guess I had my blinders on, and I agreed. A year later, Carly was born, so I became pretty busy."

"I'll bet."

She could see the questions in his eyes—the question of what happened to her marriage. And why, after so many years, was she still single.

But he didn't ask those questions. Instead, he said, "Did you grow up with a garden?"

"Not at my house. My grandfather gardened, and I helped him a lot. Hated to stay around the house when both my parents were home. They had one of those marriages that should have been a divorce. Instead, they stayed together and just fought all the time."

Wyatt grimaced. "Sorry."

"Mom." Carly's voice sounded from the house. "How long are you going to be? I'm making popcorn to go with your cookies."

"We're being summoned," Anita said with an apologetic smile.

"Sounds like it." Wyatt glanced around them. "Maybe we can finish the tour another time."

"There's not much else." She stepped back onto the path she'd created with white gravel.

"Oh, I have lots of questions," he said, following her.

She laughed. "I don't think a kindergartener has as many questions as you."

"You might be right," he said, his tone warm, "but this is all out of my depth, so it's kind of fascinating."

Anita had to focus on not walking awkwardly after that. His compliments were subtle, but seemed sincere. As they neared the house, she smelled cooking popcorn. "I guess she's still hungry. Brownies just don't cut it."

Wyatt chuckled.

Inside the house, Carly stood next to the stove, pouring kernels of corn into a pan with sizzling oil. She stirred the mixture with a wooden spoon, then set the lid on it and turned down the element. The first kernel popped.

Anita found a bowl for the popcorn, then opened the refrigerator. "What would you like to drink, Wyatt?" she asked. "We have cream soda, water, milk."

"It's powdered milk," Carly shot out. "You should pass on it."

He paused by the counter. "Water's fine."

"You can't have water with popcorn," Carly said. "You have to have cream soda."

"Carly—he can have water," Anita started.

"I'll have the cream soda, then," Wyatt said with a smile. "You're a persuasive young lady."

Carly only grinned, and Anita pulled out three cream sodas.

Soon, they'd all settled at the table, popcorn between them. Wyatt turned to Carly. "Since you have the best handwriting here, can you be the scribe?"

The Healing Garden

Anita raised her brows. How he knew anything about her handwriting was a mystery, but she pulled the notepad toward her, looking very pleased.

"Now," he said, "we should start with the phone book and call all the Martins in the area."

"What are we going to say to them?" Anita asked.

"What if no one wants to give out information?" Carly added.

"We hope they'll want to help an elderly man find his old high school friend," Wyatt said.

The next hour they took turns making phone calls. Even Carly made one of the calls. But they kept hitting dead ends. The sky outside darkened with rain clouds, and soon it started to drizzle, making the world turn gray.

Anita turned on a couple of lights. "Do you think we could ask the city office where Susan lived in Nevada to mail phone records of any Martins they have?"

"It's worth a try." Wyatt dialed information, then asked for the number. Next he called the city office.

Through the receiver, Anita could hear a woman's voice answer. Wyatt explained why he was calling. "Anything would help. My grandfather is hoping to reconnect with Susan Martin. She'd be about eighty-three right now."

He paused, then said, "They dated, yes."

Anita decided that his side of the conversation was getting interesting.

"I believe they were in love," he continued, a small smile appearing on his face.

Carly drew a heart in the notepad.

"Yeah, I suppose it's a sweet story. Gramps is very eager, that's all I know." He chuckled and glanced over at Anita. "Great, that would be excellent. Thank you so much." He rattled off his home address, then hung up a moment later.

When his gaze again met Anita's, he said, "Well, she's intrigued and will mail us whatever she can find about any Martins in that city."

"Wow, that's great," she said. "She was very helpful."

Carly's eyes glowed. "She's excited about the romance. When you told her about that, she wanted to help more."

Wyatt nodded, his smile growing. "I believe you're right." His gaze again connected with Anita, and she wondered if it was time to get everyone more drinks—with ice.

"Now what do we do?" Carly asked, tapping her pencil against the notepad.

"We wait for Ms. Anderson to send over what she finds." Wyatt folded his hands on the table. "Unless there's something else you can think of?"

"We should type up form letters," Carly suggested. "You know, so that when we get names, and if some of the people don't want to talk on the phone, we can send them letters."

Anita's brows popped up. "That's a great idea, Carly."

"I agree," Wyatt said. "What should the letters say?"

Anita guessed he was including Carly in the process as much as possible, because surely he could compose a letter. Over the next hour, they put together a letter they were all happy with. Anita typed up a few versions, and only had to use Wite-Out a few times to correct errors.

"You should stay for dinner," Carly said. "My mom's a good cook, and I always help too."

Anita's mouth nearly fell open. First that she was inviting Wyatt to dinner, and next that Carly thought she was a good cook. She hadn't really planned out a meal, and now her mind raced with what to say.

"I don't want to impose," Wyatt said, but he was looking at Anita.

What could she say? "It's no problem. Don't expect anything fancy."

The Healing Garden

"We can have spaghetti," Carly declared. "Do we have everything for that?"

"Yes, we do." She exhaled. "It's easy enough, and we'd be happy to have you."

"Only if you let me make the sauce," Wyatt said. "I have a special recipe."

His smile was easy, and she suddenly felt nervous. Working together on finding Susan was one thing, but sharing a meal in her home made everything feel a lot more domestic.

"It's a deal," Carly said. "I'll do the salad. I make them a lot."

"Sounds great," he said.

Carly pushed up from the table and headed to the refrigerator.

"Are you sure it's okay?" Wyatt asked in a quiet voice, his gaze not letting her look anywhere else.

"It's fine," Anita replied. "Like Carly said, spaghetti is easy, and it's nice to have company."

"Nice for me too."

She wasn't sure how to read into that, and she only grew more curious about his life and relationships. "I'm just glad Carly likes you so much. Less butting heads."

"I'm glad too." Wyatt stood and headed to the row of cupboards. "Can you show me where the spices are?" he asked Carly.

Anita watched him for a moment, interacting with her daughter in their kitchen. It all seemed so . . . foreign, yet normal at the same time. She felt like she was looking in through a window at some other family that wasn't hers, as a man and his daughter bantered in the kitchen while they cooked. Anita gave a small shake of her head. She couldn't let those thoughts enter her mind right now. She wasn't looking for a relationship. And Carly didn't need the complication of more than what she was already dealing with.

Anita stood and joined them in the kitchen, pulling out the pots—one for the sauce, one for the pasta. In the next little while, she found out that Wyatt liked to whistle, that he was particular about spaghetti sauce, and that his presence somehow made her home full of bright sunshine despite the rain outside.

Fifteen

ANITA HADN'T REALIZED SHE'D MISS Wyatt Davis so much. For the past two weeks, she and Carly had visited Mr. Davis, but never when Wyatt was there. He'd called once, about a week ago, just to say he was still waiting for the mailings to come from Nevada. They'd agreed that when it arrived, they'd set another time to get together.

Phyllis had brought up Wyatt at their shared lunches, when they were sitting on the back patio overlooking one of their gardens. But Anita maintained they were friends and that she didn't have any extra information to offer. Besides, she wasn't going to spill any of the thoughts circulating in her head about the man anyway.

But when the phone rang a short time after one of the lunches, she answered to hear Wyatt's voice on the phone. She knew immediately why he'd called.

"You received records from the city office?" she asked.

"I did." Wyatt's voice was warm, deep, and made her stomach do a little somersault.

"Anything look interesting?"

"It's hard to tell without making the calls," he said. "But there's more here than I expected."

"Ms. Anderson really came through," Anita mused.

He chuckled. "She really did." He paused. "What's your schedule like in the next few days?"

She walked over to the calendar on the wall. She knew the schedule, but looking at the date boxes with the handwritten details in them helped her focus. "Carly started in the school band and has practice three days a week after school."

"Oh, that's great she's involved with band. What does she play?"

Anita smiled at his enthusiasm. "Uh, the french horn for now. It's all new. She's doing it with those new friends she made."

"Were you in band?"

"No." She laughed. "I was an art geek. What about you?"

"Uh, no musical talent for me."

She waited, and when he didn't continue, she said, "What did you do in high school?"

She heard his sigh on the other end. "Cross country."

She could easily picture him running. He probably still ran. That would explain his lean physique. "Oh, do you still run?"

"I do."

"I don't think you could pay me to run for fun," she said, twisting the phone cord around her fingers. "The last time I ran was for a PE class in high school."

"You probably didn't give it a chance," he said. "The more you run, the more you want to do it."

"That makes no sense."

Wyatt laughed, warm and deep. "It's too hard to convince someone unless they actually try it."

Anita found herself smiling. "I hope you don't think I'm willing to be your guinea pig, because I'm not."

"Suit yourself."

She was still smiling when she hung up with Wyatt. They'd agreed to meet that afternoon. Carly wouldn't have band, so it would work out time-wise. It wasn't that she had to be with them, but she'd be upset if she were left out. She'd asked multiple times over the past two weeks for updates.

Anita grabbed her keys and decided some grocery shopping was in order. Just in case Wyatt stayed for dinner again. She headed to the store, grateful for the sunny day. Everything seemed brighter for some reason. The colors of the vibrant green bushes, the scarlet blooms, a shiny sky-blue car . . . She didn't realize she was smiling to herself until an older woman pushing a cart full of potato rolls greeted her in the grocery aisle.

"You're having a good day," the woman said in a friendly tone.

She blinked. "I guess I am."

The woman nodded and continued on her way. Anita looked about the aisle, not sure what exactly she wanted to fix for dinner. She headed to the meats section and decided on stir fry. She had the time to marinate the meat. Next, she picked up salad fixings, then paused by the bin with corn on the cob. She wondered if Wyatt liked corn. She picked up a few, deciding that most people liked corn.

"Anita?" a man said from behind her.

The back of her neck prickled. She'd know that voice anywhere. Yet it was impossible to hear it in her local grocery store. Maybe she'd misheard another person talking.

"It is you," the man continued, coming around the other side of the bin.

Anita's heart sank as she looked into the brown eyes of her ex-husband. "Bobby?"

"Robert. I go by Robert now." His brows pulled together as he studied her.

She studied him right back. His dark brown hair was short, with a hint of gray at the temples. He wore a brand-name golf shirt that sat snug around his stomach paunch, revealing the weight he'd gained over the years, but clearly he'd never changed his shirt size. A gold chain winked at his neck, and he wore one of those watches that looked expensive. Even from here, she could smell his dose of cologne. It had been a long time since she'd seen this man . . . how long exactly? Ten years.

"What are you doing in . . . Seattle?" she managed to ask.

"You're looking really good, Anita." Bobby's open gaze perused her as if he had all the time in the world to be staring at her in a grocery store.

"What are you doing in Seattle?" she repeated.

His eyes flicked back to her face, and he flashed his white smile. "I'm visiting my parents."

She nodded and gripped the handle of her shopping cart. "How are they?"

"Fine." His brows quirked. "Where's Carly?"

She felt immediately annoyed by the question. "She's at school, Bobby. With all the other kids her age."

"Right, right." He rubbed a hand over his chin, which had some stubble.

She'd forgotten him always saying his little catchphrase of *Right, right.*

"Are you single?"

Anita opened her mouth, then closed it. This man had no right to any information about her personal life. Especially not after completely disappearing from Carly's life. Instead of answering, she said, "Are you still married?"

His gaze flicked with something unreadable. "Gloria and I are separated."

Gloria . . . had Anita ever known his second wife's name? "Sorry to hear that," she said stiffly. How else was she supposed to reply?

The Healing Garden

"You didn't answer my question." He gave that white smile again—the one in which he expected to always get his way.

Why couldn't there be some sort of interruption? Maybe another person needing to pick out corn? Or an announcement about a sale on cucumbers coming over the PA system? Or maybe she could have arrived at the store fifteen minutes later and avoided all of this. "I'm still single," she said.

He nodded as if he weren't surprised at all. "That makes things easier," he said, moving a few steps around the corn bin.

"Makes *what* easier?"

"Visiting Carly," Bobby said. "I miss her."

Anita wanted to laugh. Or cry. "How long has that been going on?"

He cocked his head. "What? Missing my daughter? I've missed her since the day we parted ways."

Anita folded her arms. "Carly hasn't seen you in *ten years*, Bobby. And don't tell me a couple of cruddy birthday cards count."

For the first time, he looked uncomfortable. His brows tugged together as he rubbed the back of his neck. "Things have been very busy and complicated. I'm sure you understand."

"Not really." Anita's mind raced as she wondered what Bobby was really about. Was he going to contact Carly, then ditch her again? Would it be better if there were no contact at all? Anita didn't have the legal right to keep them apart since they technically had joint custody, although he'd never taken his half seriously.

"I've never skipped child support," he continued. "So you can't paint me as a deadbeat dad."

Anita had so many responses to that, but she only spoke one of them. "Carly doesn't even know you, and you don't know her. So I guess that speaks for itself."

Bobby's gaze shifted to the floor. Had she really gotten through to him? And if he missed their daughter so much, why had he been so AWOL? When he raised his gaze, she saw a flash of who he used to be when they were younger. She pushed back any affectionate memories.

"Look, when I was with Gloria and her kids, things were tricky. If I even brought up visiting Carly, I'd get the cold shoulder for days. And when I came to visit my parents, she came too. I could have at least sent more cards, but I kept hoping I could visit in person."

Anita stared at him for a moment, wondering if he was sincere. Was she supposed to believe that Gloria was so cruel as to keep a man from his kid?

Bobby lifted a hand. He still wore his wedding ring. "Look, why don't I give you my parents' number. You can talk to Carly, and if she wants to see me, have her call me. That way we can go by her schedule."

It actually sounded kind of fair. Anita would never keep Carly away from her own father, but there were definitely going to be emotions. And she would support her daughter's decision; she was old enough to know her own mind.

"All right."

Bobby's expression brightened, and his smile returned. "Great. Let me find something to write the number on." He fished a wallet out of his back pocket.

"It's fine," Anita said. "I already know that number. Unless it's changed?"

He paused. "No, it's the same. In fact, nothing about their house has changed. Not the furniture, not the faded pink flamingos in the flower beds, and not the bent red flag on the mailbox."

The Healing Garden

Anita shared a smile with him, something she didn't know was still possible. "How are they? Still healthy?" It was a personal question, she knew, but she wanted as much information about Bobby and his family as possible before turning Carly over to them.

"Mom's great. Staying busy as usual fussing over everything and everyone. Dad has diabetes now, so he's trying to adjust to that. He's not much for exercise, so Mom's trying to get him to take walks about the neighborhood when it's not raining."

"What about mall walking?"

"*Mall* walking?" He stared at her as if she'd suddenly broken out into a foreign language.

"Yes, it's popular with seniors," Anita said. "The malls open extra early for people who want to walk the mall. The stores aren't open yet, but you don't have to worry about weather issues."

"Interesting," he said. "I had no idea."

She shrugged. "Your dad might like it."

"Thanks, I'll tell him about it." Bobby paused. "I might be the one driving them to the mall. Neither of them like to drive too far out of town."

"I understand."

Bobby seemed to run out of steam, or conversation. He suddenly looked antsy, shifting from one foot to the other. "I've got to get back home." He nodded to the basket at his feet with a few groceries inside. "Mom is waiting."

A surreal moment to be sure, since when they were in high school, the last place Bobby spent any time was home. His parents were strict and conventional and stuffy. They'd never liked Anita—an artist—but she also knew that their divorce was completely disgraceful in their eyes.

"I'll talk to Carly and let you know what she says," she

said, even though she dreaded the conversation with her daughter. Maybe it would be all right, though. Years had passed, and soon enough Carly would be an adult and would have to eventually figure out her relationship with her father.

"Thank you, I appreciate it," Bobby said in a perfectly polite tone. His gaze moved over her for a few seconds. "It was great to see you, Anita. I'm glad you're doing well."

He hadn't even asked her how she was doing and didn't ask her anything personal. She wasn't surprised, and she didn't want to tell him anything personal either. He'd always been that way—only focused on his own interests and needs. She supposed that in high school she was charmed by his daredevil personality. He was good-looking, and half the girls in school had a crush on him. So Anita had been flattered when he picked her out of the crowd.

A short time into their marriage, she realized he was really only interested in her when she made him look good or complimented him. He'd been attracted to her artsy personality since it was so opposite of his own upbringing, and he probably knew it would drive his parents crazy. Which it had.

Having a baby and wife at home had been too restricting. Too boring. He'd started to prioritize his friends over her, and that's when things between them crumbled. She grew up, and he didn't. That he'd married another woman with a kid was kind of ironic. Except Gloria lived the fast life too. Apparently she was all right with nannies and babysitters—not to further a career or go on a couple's vacation with her husband, but to live a full nightlife as if she didn't have a kid who needed a parent.

Anita knew she shouldn't judge, but she supposed she was anyway. Especially because it was that type of mindset that had broken up her marriage. Or at least in part. If it weren't for Carly missing out on a father, she would have been happy to have her relationship with Bobby over. Their dating in high school was fun and exciting, but for her, that didn't translate to the rigors of adult life and responsibility.

Still . . . as Bobby walked away, she could see how much he'd changed. Physically especially. They all aged at some point, Anita decided. They all matured, and hopefully for the better. Maybe he would follow through with Carly. Maybe they could have a new beginning.

Turning back to the produce section, she stood for a few moments, unseeing. Emotions warred in her chest, and she couldn't remember what she was planning on fixing for dinner. Then she remembered the corn. She loaded up on a few ears. She could do something normal like fixing dinner. And tonight, after Wyatt left, she would have a talk with Carly.

Somehow the rest of the afternoon passed, and it was time for Wyatt to arrive at her house. He was on time, and she found herself analyzing him as he came up the walk, carrying a box. She liked him, she knew that. Was this how it was with Bobby when she first met him? No, she told herself. Bobby had been a flashy personality—popular at school. Wyatt was subdued, serious, solid. Bobby wore his heart on his sleeve, whereas Wyatt showed his heart through his actions, his concern.

"Stop comparing them," Anita scolded herself in a fierce whisper.

She opened the door for Wyatt, and he carried in the box.

"Wow, it is a lot of stuff," she said.

"Yeah, I was surprised too." He paused in the entryway, his eyes locking on her. "How's your week going?"

"All right." She knew it was just a casual question, but

Wyatt always seemed to see her. To listen to her. To want to know more. "How was your week?"

"Better now." He lifted the box a couple of inches. "Should I put this on the kitchen table?"

"Yes, sure." She shut the door and followed him into the kitchen, where he set the box down.

He began pulling out folders. "Smells good in here."

"Oh." Anita moved to the other side of the table. "I have some meat marinating, so you're probably smelling the sauce. It's pretty strong."

"Ah." He fished out another folder.

"And you're welcome to stay for dinner," she said. "Carly will probably ask you."

Wyatt set down the folder he held, the edge of his mouth lifting. "You don't have to feed me."

She gave a small shrug. "I don't mind. The more the merrier."

"I should have brought something. Dessert, at least."

"It's fine. I'm actually making a new recipe. Something I've wanted to try for a while. And the portion is too much for two people."

Wyatt's brows raised. "I'm happy to be your taste tester anytime."

Anita might be blushing, even though she knew he wasn't teasing her *that* way.

"Hey, is everything all right?" he asked suddenly. "If tonight's not a good time, we can reschedule."

"Oh yeah, things are fine."

"Are *you* all right?" he pressed. "You seem . . . stressed?"

She folded her arms because her hands felt shaky, and her heart was beating too hard. Would it be terrible to tell Wyatt what happened today? Maybe it would be good to have an outsider's opinion. It wasn't something she'd discuss with any of her neighbors or clients. "I ran into Carly's dad today. We haven't seen or heard from him in years. He's back in town staying at his parents'."

"Wow. That's a lot."

"Yeah, and he wants to see Carly. So I'm telling her tonight." Anita didn't mean for the tears to fall. She hadn't cried over Bobby in a long time.

"Hey," Wyatt said in a soft voice. He walked around the table and pulled her into his arms.

She hadn't expected him to hug her, and she hadn't known how badly she needed a hug. Someone's arms holding her, someone caring about how she felt, someone comforting her. It was nice.

"Sorry," she whispered, wiping at her eyes. "I didn't expect to blubber about it."

He gave a soft chuckle. "You can blubber on me anytime."

Anita drew away and met his gaze. "I'm sure you don't mean that, but you're very gallant for offering."

Wyatt released her, smoothing a bit of hair from her face before stepping away. "Gallantry has nothing to do with my offer. I've been heartbroken before, so I want you to know there's no judgment on my part. These things take time."

Sixteen

IF CARLY HADN'T WALKED THROUGH the door at that moment, Anita would have asked Wyatt who'd broken his heart. She knew he hadn't been married, so was it a serious relationship? At least wondering about it was a distraction from Bobby. As she watched Wyatt interact with Carly, and how she seemed perfectly happy right now, Anita steeled herself for that changing.

"Where do we start first?" Carly asked as she munched on an apple. Sassy had parked herself on Carly's lap. "That's a lot of phone calls if we call everyone on those lists."

Wyatt tapped one of the lists. "I put an asterisk by the ones I think we should start with. See their residency dates? They're the ones who lived in the town the longest."

"Good plan." Carly took another bite of her apple.

A memory stirred about Bobby as Anita watched her. They used to meet for library study sessions, and he always sneaked in snacks. It was a challenge for her to not get caught. She blinked the memory away.

"Okay, let's do this." Carly pointed at the first name. "Let's call Mr. Leo Martin."

Wyatt pulled the phone closer to him and dialed, then lifted the receiver to his ear. After several moments, he said, "No answer."

Carly wrote "CB" next to the man's name for "call back." "What about Alice Martin?"

The Healing Garden

Wyatt dialed the next number. "Alice Martin?" he said into the phone. "This is Wyatt Davis and—" He moved the receiver from his ear and looked at Anita. "She hung up."

Carly shrugged and wrote "CB" next to the woman's name. "Maybe Mom or me can try her later. She probably thought you were one of those Kirby vacuum sales guys."

Wyatt chuckled. "Probably."

"Can I try the next one?" Carly asked.

Wyatt looked as surprised as Anita felt. "Sure. Go for it."

She dialed, and as she waited for Marjorie Martin to pick up the phone, Wyatt met Anita's gaze. "You okay?" he mouthed.

She couldn't explain the expansion of her heart. "I'm okay," she mouthed back.

"Hi, Mrs. Martin?" Carly said in a rather professional tone.

Anita raised her brows, very interested to see how this conversation was going to go.

"My name is Carly Gifford, and I'm helping my friend's grandpa find a long-lost friend." She paused, her nose wrinkling. "No, it's not a school fundraiser. How old am I? Fourteen."

Another pause. "I actually live in Seattle, but the friend moved to your city in 1919." Carly nodded. "Yeah, I know it was a long time ago. The woman is Susan Martin, and she'd be about eighty-three right now."

Anita smiled, impressed with her daughter, no matter the outcome of this phone call. Wyatt reached over and squeezed her hand, his smile wide, too.

"Oh, you do?" Carly said, reaching for a pencil. "But she moved away?"

Anita covered her mouth and stared at her. Did they already have a lead?

"Do you know where?" she continued. "No? Do you know if she got married before leaving?" She scribbled something illegible on the paper. "Okay, well, is there anything else you can remember that might help my friend and his grandpa?"

Another moment passed, then Carly said, "Thank you very much, Mrs. Martin." She hung up and wrote down another sentence on the paper.

"Well?" Anita asked, too impatient to wait. "What did she say?"

Carly lifted her gaze. "She said she knew a Susan Martin who used to work at a grocery store. She moved away, though, when they were about twenty years old. If it really was the Susan we're looking for, she didn't marry before leaving Carson, Nevada."

Wyatt frowned. "That might make things easier—if we don't have to figure out her married name. But Gramps said she was engaged the last he heard, so she must have ended up somewhere with a husband."

"Let's keep calling," Anita said. "We at least have more information now to work with."

Over the next hour, they made several phone calls, until they hit the jackpot. Almost literally.

"Jack Martin," Anita said, pointing to the next name on the list. "He's been in that town for thirty years."

"Born there?" Wyatt asked.

"Maybe . . ."

"Could be a nephew." He began to dial the number.

She listened as Wyatt introduced himself, and then his eyes widened. He grabbed the pencil and began to write. "You're saying that Susan Martin is your aunt?" He paused, his gaze shifting to Anita and Carly, then back to the notebook. "Where is she now?"

The Healing Garden

Wyatt closed his eyes as he listened to Jack's reply.

Anita wished she could hear what he was saying, but all she could hear was his murmured voice.

Wyatt opened his eyes and began to write more things down. "Do you happen to have her address? Or phone number?"

Anita's mind spun. Susan was alive and reachable. Amazement and gratitude flooded through her. What would it be like when they told Mr. Davis?

Moments later, Wyatt hung up. He drew in a slow breath, then said, "Susan is in Medford, Oregon."

"Where the postcard came from?"

He nodded. "She's living with her daughter, Lila. She divorced a long time ago, I guess."

"So she did marry . . ." Anita cleared her throat. "How's her health?"

A line appeared between Wyatt's brows. "Her nephew said that she is healthy physically, but she's had some mental struggles. She's basically a recluse. She's agoraphobic and doesn't leave the house."

Anita said nothing, but Carly's brows popped up. "Why won't she leave the house?"

"It's part of a mental illness," Wyatt said.

"Maybe something bad happened to her?" Carly suggested. "To make her afraid?"

"I honestly don't know a lot about agoraphobia," he said.

"I don't either," Anita said. "Did her nephew say anything else?"

"Yeah." Wyatt tapped the paper. "He said I could call her. Maybe introduce myself before I give any information to Gramps. Test the waters, so to speak."

"Do you think she wants to be contacted?" Anita asked.

"It's hard to say." He retraced the phone number with his pencil. "She did send that postcard."

"With no return address." Anita hesitated. "Does she have any other issues, like dementia?"

"Not that Jack knows of," Wyatt said. "He spoke to her a couple of months ago."

Anita nodded and stared at the number and address he had written down. "Well?"

"What are you thinking?" he asked in a tentative tone.

"We should call her right now!" Carly said.

Wyatt rubbed his forehead. "I'm thinking that too. If we're all ready to do this?"

Carly raised her hand into the air. "I'm ready!"

Anita smiled and Wyatt chuckled.

"All right, here we go . . ." He linked his fingers and stretched out his hands, then picked up the receiver.

Anita moved over a seat to be right next to him, and Carly scooted her chair closer.

They could hear the ringing of the phone, and then a woman answered it. "Lila Martin?" he said. "This is Wyatt Davis, I'm the grandson of Sam Davis, an old friend of your mother's. My grandpa has been hoping to get in touch with her."

The woman didn't say anything for a moment, and Wyatt moved the receiver out a few inches from his ear, so Carly and Anita could listen in.

Finally, the woman spoke, her voice sounding sharp through the receiver. "Sam Davis? From Seattle?"

"Yes, that's right." Wyatt gave Carly a thumbs-up. "I guess your mother sent him a postcard a few months ago, and hearing from her brought back a lot of memories."

The woman took a long moment to answer again. "I told her not to send that postcard, but I guess she found a way to without me knowing it."

The Healing Garden

Wyatt blinked. "I'm sorry. Is there a reason you don't want her to get in touch with my grandpa?"

Lila didn't hesitate this time. "Yes. He broke her heart decades ago, and she never got over it. She has to move on, *needs* to move on. It's been over sixty years, as you know."

"It has been a long time," Wyatt agreed. "But *she* moved from Seattle with her family. From what I heard, there was no other option. So I don't see how she can say that my grandpa broke her heart."

"That's her story to tell," Lila said. "But I don't want her upset all over again."

"I understand." Wyatt drew in a breath. "Would it be possible to speak with her? Maybe it would actually be healing?"

Lila scoffed. "Her life has been far from easy. All those promises made to her by Sam Davis were broken, and I'm not going to watch her suffer over it one more day."

"I'm really sorry for all of her pain," Wyatt said. "Do you think it will help her to talk through all of this? I can have my grandpa call her."

"No," Lila said. "I don't know how you got this number, but I don't want to ever hear from your grandpa."

Anita touched his arm. "Give her your number," she whispered.

He nodded. "I got this number from Jack Martin. I didn't mean to stir up painful feelings or memories. Could you please write down my number in case . . . in case you do happen to change your mind and speak to her?"

He paused, then finally he recited his phone number. When he hung up, he rubbed at both temples. "What happened that Gramps isn't telling us?"

Anita laid a hand on his arm. "I don't know, but it sounds like Susan was very hurt by it."

Wyatt nodded. "Yeah. I don't know either—Gramps made everything sound like they wanted to see each other again, but circumstances never worked out. Then they both married, and fell out of touch."

"Do you think your grandpa forgot what happened between them?" Carly asked.

"Possibly," he acknowledged. "But obviously Susan hasn't. Maybe it's better we tell Gramps that we couldn't find her. The truth might hurt too much."

"Or be healing," Carly said. "Isn't that what you told Lila?"

"It is," Wyatt said. "And I know we can't keep this from Gramps, but it worries me too." He met Anita's gaze. "Are we opening a can of worms by doing this?"

Carly rose from the table. "I vote we call Susan's house again another night. Maybe she'll answer. Maybe her daughter is protecting her for a reason that doesn't matter anymore. Susan wrote to your grandpa, after all."

Wyatt's brows shot up. "Are you sure you're only fourteen?"

She smiled. "Yep, and I'm starving. Let's get dinner ready."

"I'm in." Wyatt rose from the table too, and as Carly headed into the kitchen, he turned to Anita. "What do you think? Should we continue down this path?"

She drew in a breath. "I agree with Carly. Your grandpa keeps talking about her. And maybe he broke her heart, but they can work through it, right? It's never too late?"

Wyatt gave a thoughtful nod. "Right." He peered at her. "Are you sure you want to keep helping me? I mean, you have a lot on your plate with talking to Carly later."

"Honestly, this has helped her with a larger perspective on life." She stood. "And as for the other . . . I have to trust that Carly will be able to handle her father."

The Healing Garden

Wyatt's gaze moved over her face. "If there's anything I can help with, let me know."

"Of course."

He grasped her hand, his touch warm and gentle at the same time. "I mean it, Anita. I want to help. You've both helped me along this tricky road. I would have ignored it if not for Carly."

She smiled, but mostly her stomach fluttered at the way he held her hand. It was short-lived, of course, because Carly was only a dozen feet away in the kitchen. "All right, I'll let you know. Thanks for the offer."

Wyatt stepped away from her, and they both headed into the kitchen.

"What can I do?" he asked.

"Cut these up." Carly handed over a couple of peppers.

"Orange peppers?"

"They're sweet," Anita said. "Do you think you can handle an onion, too?"

"Bring it on." Wyatt smiled. "I can't promise not to cry, though."

Once the meat and veggies were sizzling in the wok, Carly said, "I think we should tell your grandpa all about what Lila said. Then we'll see what his answer is."

Wyatt paused where he was setting napkins on the table. "You're right. The more I think about it, the more curious I am. Don't you think it's odd that Susan would claim he broke her heart?"

"Or maybe Lila is just dramatic?" Carly offered. "Like some of my friends."

"That's a long time to hold on to a heartbreak, though," Anita said.

Carly shrugged and sat down at the kitchen table. "Not so long. I mean, divorced couples hate each other for the rest of their lives."

Anita stilled. "Where did you hear that?"

Carly looked up. "No one. It's just what I observed. You hate Dad. And my friend Becky said that her parents have been divorced for five years, and they still hate each other."

Anita wondered what Wyatt was thinking about all of this. "I don't hate your father, Carly. I just hate that he disappeared on us." Of course that could all change now. "Can we talk about this later? I don't want to spoil our dinner." Maybe putting off a teenager's caustic remarks wasn't the best parenting move, but she couldn't keep up with the conversation with Wyatt here. There was too much to talk to Carly about, and it needed to be done in private.

"Anyone want some rice?" Anita scooped rice from the pan into a serving bowl.

"I do," both Wyatt and Carly said.

The next half-hour was spent eating and chatting, with Anita steering the conversation to things like the school band and her newest art client. Wyatt even talked a little about his day at work.

All too soon, dinner was over. They all agreed to meet at the assisted living center the following night and talk to Mr. Davis. Wyatt gathered up his files and headed to the door, and Carly disappeared into her bedroom to call one of her new friends.

Wyatt paused at the front door. "I guess we didn't need so much information after all when Jack Martin turned out to be a direct link."

"We got lucky," Anita said. For some reason, she didn't want him to leave yet. Because when he did, she'd have no more excuses to put off talking to Carly about her dad.

"Call me later?" Wyatt said, his green eyes on her.

She hesitated, and he rushed to say, "Or not. But I'll be hoping the best for your talk with Carly."

The Healing Garden

"I'll call you." Her pulse sped up. "I don't want you home alone dying to know what's going on."

His mouth lifted. "That perfectly describes what I'll be going through if you don't call."

Anita folded her arms. "So . . . you mentioned that you've been through heartbreak. What happened?"

Surprise crossed his expression. "You remember?"

"I do."

He glanced away for a second, then said, "Her name was Cynthia. She basically left me at the altar—well, I did get a few hours' notice, so I wasn't actually standing at the altar."

"Oh, I'm sorry." She winced. "How long ago did that happen?"

"Three years." He shifted the box in his hands. "Long enough to be over the rejection, but not long enough to completely forget it."

Anita could see the pain in his eyes . . . He'd obviously really cared for Cynthia. "I'm sorry. It sounds like a rough breakup."

Wyatt nodded. "The long view is that it was for the best. And life moves on. And sometimes there's something better waiting."

Seventeen

ANITA AWAKENED THE FOLLOWING MORNING after a restless night. She hadn't slept much, and it wasn't because of her talk with Carly. That had actually gone much better than she could have predicted. Carly was both curious and wary about her father being in town and wanting to connect with her. In fact, she'd called him last night, and they chatted for about ten minutes.

Anita heard her half of the conversation, and after it was over, Carly simply said, "He's going to visit on Friday. I'm not ready to go do anything with him, but I told him he could come over and visit."

Anita thought that was a good idea. A baby step. Not that she was looking forward to having Bobby in her home—looking things over—but this was about her daughter. And she had to focus on that.

What surprised her, though, was the phone call she received around lunchtime from Wyatt. Thankfully Phyllis wasn't over that day. His warm voice coming through the phone somehow settled her circling thoughts.

"How are you?" he asked.

It was a common enough question, but coming from Wyatt, she knew it was genuine.

"I'm doing all right," she said. "Are you on lunch break?"

The Healing Garden

"I am, and I guess I was too curious to wait for when you were going to call me."

"Oh, I was going to call you, huh?"

He chuckled. "Am I being too transparent?"

She sat at the kitchen table. "I think you need to be more transparent after a statement like that."

She could hear the smile in his voice when he replied, "You're a taskmaster, Anita. I'm sure that comes with being a parent, but also being both an artist and a businesswoman."

"Ah, starting out with the compliments, I see."

"Is it working?"

She smiled to herself. "I won't turn any down."

"Good." Wyatt paused. "I don't want to pull any punches, Anita. I like you and I've enjoyed spending time together."

Anita wondered at the depth of his words, but goose bumps broke out on her arms anyway. "I like you too, Wyatt."

"I think you just made my day."

She touched her cheek. Sure enough, it was plenty hot.

"How did the talk with Carly go?" he asked.

"Surprisingly well." Anita didn't mind his questions, so she updated him on the conversation and the outcome. "He's coming to visit Carly tomorrow night at our house."

"How do you feel about that?"

She winced. "Uh . . . can I plead the Fifth?"

Wyatt laughed. "You certainly can. Although pleading the Fifth pretty much makes your opinion clear."

"Well, I'm telling myself it's all good, and that it won't turn out too good to be true."

"Do you think your ex will flake out?"

"He could, or maybe he will later. You know, visit a handful of times, then disappear again." She wrapped the phone cord around her fingers. "I just don't want to see Carly disappointed."

"Yeah, I get it. She's a great kid, and I'd think any man would be proud to have her as a daughter."

Anita's heart twisted at his kind words. "Thank you. I believe that as well, but I also know that not all people are wired to be attentive parents." She cut off her words, hoping she wasn't crossing the line.

"Yeah . . . I know that firsthand," he said softly.

"I'm sorry, Wyatt, I didn't mean to bring that up."

"It's fine. I shared about my mom with you and Carly, and I'm glad I did. I wanted her to know that there are a lot of people out there who are dealing with hard things."

Anita still felt bad about bringing up something that must be painful.

"I've made peace with my parent-less life because I've realized how blessed I've been with such steadfast grandparents."

"Your grandpa is a sweet man," Anita said, glad that she'd sidestepped a landmine. "And I'm sure your grandma was wonderful, too."

"She really was." Wyatt's tone remained subdued. "Are we still on for meeting at the center tonight? I'd love to have you and Carly there. You know, to ease him into the news about Susan."

"We wouldn't miss it for the world. Six thirty, right?"

"Right—soon after dinner."

"Okay."

"Hey, should I pick you two up? It's not much out of the way."

She didn't hesitate. "Sure, that would be great. I've become fond of the red Cadillac."

Wyatt laughed. "Me too."

The Healing Garden

She was tempted to ask him to come earlier and have dinner, but maybe that would be too much...

"It's a plan, then," he said, his low voice rumbling through the phone. "I'll see you in a few hours."

After hanging up with Wyatt, Anita remained at the kitchen table for several moments, sorting through all the things in her head. Complications, for sure, but new hope too. Wyatt had brought in that hope, as well as his grandpa.

She was determined that tonight would be a good night. She'd enjoy being with Wyatt and her daughter, and finding some answers for Mr. Davis.

To pass the time, she headed into the backyard to do some mindless gardening. She saw Phyllis in her yard before the woman noticed her.

"Hi, Phyllis. How are you?"

Her neighbor didn't turn to greet her, so Anita moved closer to the fence. "Phyllis?" she said loudly.

The woman spun, reaching for the headphones she had on her ears. "Oh, I'm sorry that I didn't hear you. I'm trying out this new Walkman that my son sent me for my birthday. He sent me three cassette tapes. Do you want to try it out?"

Anita reached for the Walkman over the fence. "It's your birthday?"

"Next week," Phyllis said, "but he's not going to be able to visit. I suppose that's why he was sure to send this in advance. Pretty fancy, don't you think?"

"It's a very nice gift," Anita agreed. She pushed Play on the Walkman and slipped on the headphones. "Great sound, too."

Phyllis beamed. "I love it, and I feel so hip. You should tell Carly to come and listen when she has some extra time."

"She has one," Anita said. "But I'm sure she'd love to try yours out." She handed the Walkman back to Phyllis, and the woman proudly set it back on her ears.

Anita smiled to herself, then got busy with gardening, but it did nothing to keep her mind off Wyatt.

By the time six thirty rolled around, she was a bundle of nerves. She found Carly bouncing on her toes, waiting for the red car to pull up.

"He's finally here!" she said.

Wyatt turned into the driveway, and Carly pushed out the door.

"Hang on," Anita said with a laugh, but Carly was already halfway to the car. Anita grabbed her jacket, then closed the door and locked it.

Wyatt had stepped out of the car and opened the back door for Carly, then the passenger door, waiting for Anita.

His gaze scanned her as she approached. Maybe she'd dressed up a little more than usual. She wore a lightweight denim jumpsuit with a wide leather belt, along with kitten heels.

"Good evening," he said as she neared.

She smirked at his formality. "Good evening, Mr. Davis."

His smile appeared, and she stepped past him and slid into the passenger seat. He closed the door and walked around to the other side of the car. Carly leaned close and propped her arms on the upholstery between Anita and Wyatt.

"Guess what, Wyatt?"

"What?" he asked in a cheerful tone as he backed out of the driveway.

"My dad's in town, and I'm seeing him tomorrow night."

Wyatt cut a glance to Anita, but didn't reveal he already knew the information. She realized they hadn't discussed this possibility.

The Healing Garden

"Are you excited?" he asked.

"Yes and no."

This caught Anita's attention.

"Nervous, then?" Wyatt continued, his glance moving from the road to the rearview mirror. "It's been a while since you've seen him, right?"

Carly sighed. "Yeah. Ten years. He's probably all gray now."

Wyatt's brows popped up. "Isn't he around your mom's age?"

She shrugged. "So maybe he's not all gray, but I'll bet he looks old."

Wyatt shared another glance with Anita, and they both listened as Carly rattled on about her dad. She brought up some of her memories from when she was a kid, and Anita was both surprised and grateful at how comfortable Carly felt around Wyatt to tell him so much.

In no time at all, they were turning into the parking lot of the assisted living center.

"I'm really glad you have a chance to get to know your dad again," Wyatt said. "Family is important no matter how complicated."

Carly scrunched her nose. "That sounds like something your grandpa would say."

He laughed. "I'll take that as a compliment, then."

When they walked into the dining room where Mr. Davis waited at a table, Anita's heart tugged to see him. In moments, he'd learn that they'd been in contact with Susan, but things hadn't gone so well.

"Gramps," Wyatt said, reaching him first. He leaned down and gave him a hug.

Mr. Davis patted his back with a shaky hand, then his gaze moved to see Anita and Carly. "What a surprise. You brought friends."

Wyatt smiled. "I'm sure I don't have to introduce them."

Mr. Davis held out his hand, and Anita grasped it, then Carly did.

"We have some news about our search for Susan," Wyatt said without any more preamble. "Can we talk in your room? Or someplace more private?"

Mr. Davis reached for his walker. "You heard from her?" He pushed himself up, and Wyatt reached to support him. "Let's go to the atrium. It's a nice enough night."

And it was. The weather was mild and the sky clear of most clouds, with the sunset painting it a deep orange.

"That sounds great," Wyatt said.

Their small group moved through the dining room, then outside, where there was a walled-in garden area.

"There's a couple of benches at the end of this path," Mr. Davis continued.

The fragrance of flowers bloomed about them, and Anita was impressed that the center had such a place. It was surely a refuge for the residents. "No one else is out here?" she asked.

"They're all settling in for movie night," Mr. Davis said.

"What are they watching?" Carly asked.

"I think it's one of the videos they've shown a dozen times. It's either *Somewhere in Time* or *9 to 5*," he said. "I don't pay much attention because I'd rather read."

Carly moved ahead and found the open circle with a couple of benches. She sat at the end of one, and Anita settled next to her.

"We have good news and not-so-good news, Gramps," Wyatt said.

Mr. Davis frowned. "I want it all. Is she still alive?"

Anita shouldn't have been surprised at the question, but it caught her off guard. Of course he'd wonder about that.

The Healing Garden

"She's alive and fairly healthy," Wyatt said. "I spoke to her daughter last night in Medford—where she's living now."

"Medford?" Mr. Davis nodded. "What do you mean by fairly healthy? Why didn't you talk to Susan?"

Wyatt cleared his throat. "Susan's daughter is named Lila, and she wouldn't let us speak to Susan. Lila has heard about you, and she doesn't have a very favorable opinion."

Mr. Davis looked confused at this. "What does that mean?"

"I'm not sure exactly."

"Lila said that you broke Susan's heart," Carly interjected, clearly too eager to let Wyatt beat around the bush.

Mr. Davis looked over at her, his brows pinched. "Broke her heart . . ." His voice was quiet. "Her daughter said this?"

Carly nodded, and Wyatt said, "Yeah, she made it sound like it was devastating and that Susan's still not over it after all these years."

Mr. Davis rocked back on the bench. "I don't understand. Susan and I were the best of friends. We dated, we were in love, yes, but life happened. We wrote to each other for years, and she completely stopped after getting engaged. I'm the one who was heartbroken." His voice trembled at the end of his speech, and he raised a shaky hand to wipe his eyes.

Anita found a tissue pack in her purse and crossed to him to hand one over. "I'm sorry," she said. "We didn't know what to make of Lila's comments, so we're hoping that you can tell us what happened."

Mr. Davis used the tissue, then raised both his hands in surrender. "I honestly don't know. I don't have that final letter anymore. When Norma and I married, we both purged our things of old girlfriends and old boyfriends. We started with a clean slate. She knew about Susan, of course, and I knew about Norma's former beau . . ." His voice trailed off and he closed his eyes.

"Gramps?" Wyatt set a hand on his shoulder. "Are you all right?"

Mr. Davis released a long breath. "I need to talk to her. I need to find out what Susan told her daughter."

Wyatt exchanged glances with Anita. She didn't have any answers . . . Lila had made her stance pretty clear.

Mr. Davis turned to his grandson. "Can you call again? Give them the number here. Ask if Susan can call me. Or her daughter is welcome to as well."

Wyatt dipped his chin. "I can try again, Gramps, but I don't know if that will just make things worse."

"It's already at its worst." Mr. Davis raised a trembling hand and rubbed his forehead. "I know my memory isn't what it used to be, but what in the world does she mean?"

Wyatt rested a hand on his grandpa's shoulder. "I don't know, Gramps."

Anita's stomach twisted into knots at the obvious distress Mr. Davis was feeling. He looked at Carly. "Can you help me write a letter to Susan? My handwriting is no longer steady."

She straightened and looked at Anita, who gave her a nod of approval. "I'd be happy to," she said to him. "When should we write it?"

"Tonight," he said in a determined voice. "Then one of you can mail it. The mail service here is slower than a snail's pace."

Wyatt's forehead creased, but he said, "All right. I can mail it tomorrow. No problem, Gramps."

So they headed inside, and Anita located some paper, an envelope, and a pen. As Mr. Davis dictated his letter to Carly, Anita sat near Wyatt.

The Healing Garden

"What do you think?" she asked quietly, so they wouldn't be overheard.

"I think a letter has a better chance than a phone call," Wyatt said. "But it still might not get past Lila."

"That's true." She sighed. "I wish Lila would have told us a little more."

He leaned back in his chair, folding his arms. "It's hard to know if this is a case of lost memories, or something that Gramps didn't realize he'd done. A miscommunication or something. Or . . . maybe he's not admitting to it?"

Anita bit her lip. "Maybe. Although it would be strange for your grandpa to forget something that obviously really hurt Susan."

Wyatt nodded, and they both watched and waited as Carly finished the letter writing. After Mr. Davis had dictated his last words, he reached for his walker. "I'm ready to turn in for the night."

"Already?" Wyatt moved to his feet. "Are you feeling all right?"

"I'm tired, son," Mr. Davis said. "I appreciate all you've done and that you were able to track down Susan. Now we just have to pray that she'll be willing to talk to me. Let me know the moment you get in touch with her daughter again."

"I will." Wyatt reached his side and grasped his elbow. "Do you need help to your room?"

"No, it looks like Ginny is taking me."

The aide arrived just then. "Everything all right? Did you have a nice visit?"

"It was an interesting visit, Ginny," Mr. Davis said in a subdued tone. "I'm ready to go my room now."

"Of course." She glanced at Wyatt.

He simply nodded. "Good night, Gramps."

Mr. Davis shuffled away, Ginny at his side, without a backward glance or any sort of goodbye.

Carly stared after him. "He's really sad."

It was a fair assessment. "Let's hope that Susan will get his letter," Wyatt said.

Carly handed it over to him. "Maybe you can send it certified mail? To be signed by the person it's addressed to?"

Wyatt's brows lifted. "That's an excellent idea."

But Anita wasn't as sure. "Would that give it too much attention and alert Lila?"

"That's true," he conceded.

"I wish we could just go visit her," Carly said. "It's not fair that Mr. Davis feels so sad about this. Why couldn't Lila be nicer?"

Anita gave her a side hug. "We probably don't know the whole story. Maybe Wyatt will have more luck contacting Lila again."

He puffed out a breath of air. "I hope I don't make her too upset by calling again. At least I can tell her I gave Gramps the message about Susan being heartbroken."

They all fell silent for a moment.

"It's not that late," Carly said. "We could call her right now. Maybe Susan will answer."

"Carly—" Anita began, but Wyatt cut in.

"That might be a good idea," he said. "We can call her tonight. Not worth losing sleep over it—for any of us."

Carly beamed. "Okay, then. We're going to our house to call. There's not much privacy here."

Wyatt looked at Anita for confirmation, and she nodded.

"Let's do it, then." He walked with them out of the center, and they loaded in his car.

Once they reached the house, Anita could only hope that Lila would give Wyatt a chance to talk and explain. Maybe . . . maybe they could speak to Susan.

They settled at the kitchen table, and he called the number from the night before. Again, Anita and Carly scooted close to hear as much as possible.

"Is this Lila?" he said when a woman answered. "This is Wyatt Davis calling again. We spoke on the phone last night."

"I told you not to call here again," Lila said.

"Please don't hang up. I have more information that you might be interested in hearing," Wyatt rushed to say.

There was a pause, then Lila spoke. "What could you possibly have to say? I already told you—"

"We spoke to my grandpa tonight and told him what you said." Wyatt's gaze connected with Anita, and she nodded for encouragement. "He doesn't have any memory of doing something that would break Susan's heart. To get to the point, he's devastated about it. He'd love more information. Either from you or Susan. He doesn't want there to be any misunderstandings." He dragged in a breath and waited.

They all waited.

Lila's words came loud and clear. "Mr. Davis, unless my mother walks over my dead body to get to the phone, she'll not be speaking with you or your grandfather."

The line clicked, and Wyatt moved the receiver from his ear. "She hung up on me."

The three of them sat in silence for a long moment.

Finally, Anita said, "We'll mail the letter and cross our fingers."

He nodded. "Exactly."

"Maybe Mr. Davis can call," Carly suggested. "Maybe Lila will listen to him."

Wyatt patted her shoulder. "I think that's a great idea. We'll see if anything comes of the letter first. Wait a week or two."

"Okay." Carly stood from the table. "Well, if you're done making phone calls, I'm going to call my friend Sara. She'll want an update."

Wyatt pushed the phone toward her. "I wish you had better news."

"Yeah, we all do." Carly picked up the phone and headed out of the kitchen, the cord trailing behind her.

"That kid is going places," Wyatt said with a soft smile, his gaze connecting with Anita's.

"She's so invested in this, I worry that she's being pushy." Anita brushed at an errant crumb on the table that had escaped dinner cleanup.

"She's not being pushy," he said. "I like that she's invested, too. It makes me feel like I'm not trying to come up with all the solutions for Gramps."

"Yeah . . . are you okay? Lila was pretty rude on the phone."

"She's upset, that's all," Wyatt said. "I don't know the whole story, but if I did, maybe we'd have more sympathy."

"True."

He rose from the table. "Well, I've hogged enough of your evening. I'm sure you have other things to do."

"Not really." Anita laughed and stood. "Well, I guess I do, but all this intrigue is so much more entertaining than starting laundry, or going through bills."

Wyatt reached for her hand and squeezed it. "Thanks again. To both you and Carly." He let go of her hand, but the warmth remained.

Anita wished he'd stay, but what excuse could she come up with? She could at least walk him to his car, so she did.

"And good luck with the ex tomorrow night," he said once they were outside.

Oh. Anita had forgotten about that. Spending time with

The Healing Garden

Wyatt and his grandpa had been a nice distraction for that reason alone. Her mind now spun with Carly's upcoming visit with her dad. "Thanks."

"And if you want to call me and talk, I'll answer the phone."

She smiled up at him, finding his eyes on her. "Okay, I might just do that. Be careful what you ask for."

"I am being careful."

His words were cryptic enough that she wasn't sure if he was flirting . . . "All right, Mr. Careful. Again, sorry about the Lila disappointment. Crossing my fingers that the letter reaches Susan."

"Thanks, Anita, really." He held up the letter.

"How many times are we going to say *thanks* tonight?"

He chuckled. Then he stepped close and pulled her into his arms.

She wasn't expecting a hug, but she was all for it. It took her a couple of seconds to get over her surprise, then she wrapped her arms about his waist.

He smelled like fresh air, and she didn't mind his arms around her either.

When he drew away, it was much too soon, and her mind was spinning for completely different reasons.

Eighteen

1923

THE APARTMENT WASN'T MUCH, BUT it was theirs. The married housing portion of college apartments only had the bare minimum, with a couch that filled most of the tiny living room. A single row of cupboards and small ice box in the kitchen. A full-sized bed that had become very crowded with a baby who preferred to sleep snuggled against one of her parents. And a shower that a person could barely turn around in.

But Sam and Norma both loved it. They'd had been married a year now, and baby Olivia was nearly six months old. Sam was absolutely besotted by her. It might have started when Norma was several months into her pregnancy, and the baby responded to his voice by kicking inside Norma's stomach. Or it might have been when he first held the infant, and Olivia stared at him as if he were the moon and the stars. Or it might have been the night when she was a week old and wouldn't settle down. Sam had walked the floor with her for hours, until they both fell asleep on the couch, Olivia cradled in his arms.

Currently, Sam was walking the floor with her relaxed against his shoulder. It was naptime, but she seemed to sense that her mother was out of the apartment. On Saturdays,

The Healing Garden

Sam took over baby care for a few hours while his wife caught up on errands that were made complicated with a baby. She'd gone to the library to return books.

When Olivia squirmed and lifted her head, Sam patted her back, "Shh, baby girl. Time to sleep now."

Her little body relaxed as he continued to gently pat her back. He began to hum, knowing that the vibrations of his chest would soothe her even more. Soon, her breathing deepened, and her fingers loosened from where they'd been gripping his shirtsleeve. Now for the transfer. He walked slowly into the bedroom, where they'd set the bassinet on the other side of the bed. Not that Olivia slept in it much. She was starting to turn over on her own, and was close to sitting up, so they really needed to invest in a crib. Or maybe borrow one? The last expense they could afford was furniture pieces.

Carefully, Sam transferred Olivia to the bassinet. She stirred, but thankfully didn't fully awaken. A missed nap would mess up her night schedule because she'd fall asleep way too early. Then the vicious cycle would begin. Sam exhaled silently and set a folded baby blanket across her. Her eyelashes fluttered, and he was struck by how much she looked like Norma. Honey-colored hair and green eyes.

Sam gazed at Olivia for a long moment. He didn't know if he could love this baby any more than he did. Not even if she were his own flesh and blood. Watching Norma in her motherhood had been a tender and sweet experience. It had brought him closer to her, and he could honestly say that he loved his wife. Whatever collision path they'd taken to get to this moment didn't matter in the long run. What mattered was that they were together now.

Someone knocked at the front door, and Sam moved out of the bedroom, shutting the door behind him. He hoped the sound wouldn't wake up Olivia. Maybe Norma had forgotten her keys? She was back earlier than he'd expected, but it would be nice to spend some quiet time together during Olivia's nap. When the child was awake, she took full attention from both of them.

Sam swung open the front door, fully prepared to see Norma. But a man stood on the porch, framed by the gray clouds beyond. A man who Sam recognized immediately. His skin went cold, and his stomach felt like he'd just plummeted off a three-story building. "David?"

"I didn't believe it when everyone told me." David wore a pressed dress shirt and black slacks. His dark hair was slicked back, shoes shined. In his hand he carried a bouquet of flowers.

It didn't take much deduction to decipher who he was here to see and why.

"I couldn't figure out why another man would take on a pregnant woman," David continued, his tone tight, his eyes perusing Sam. "But after working in California for a while, I began to miss her. I went out with a few gals, but no one was as sweet or as beautiful as my Norma. I asked around, and it seems that I was the only fella in her life. So that baby is mine, and Norma asked to make a life with *me*. And I turned her down."

Sam's blood simmered. He stepped onto the front stoop and pulled the door tightly closed behind him. Folding his arms, he said, "Don't speak about my wife like that, David."

The man had the gall to laugh. "*Wife* . . . yeah, you really did marry her. Legal and everything. I checked at the courthouse."

Sam tilted his head. "What do you want?"

David's lip curled. "I'm back for good. And I'm back to get what's rightfully mine. I don't care if you married her. That's my kid in there, and Norma's my girl."

It was Sam's turn to laugh, although his sounded bitter. "You signed away your parental rights. Norma showed me. And I've legally adopted Olivia." *Whoops.*

David's brows lifted. "*Olivia*? That's her name?"

"Norma is my wife, not your girl." Sam took a step closer. "You'd better leave now, or you'll get what's coming to you."

Again, David sized him up. "You think you can take me?"

"I can take you." He might be a college student, and David might have the physique of a mechanic, but Sam was defending his own. There was no way he'd be the one to go down.

David's chuckle was low. "As much as I'd love to get into a brawl with you, I'd rather hear what Norma has to say when she sees me."

Sam had never been so glad of his wife going on an errand. "She's not available right now."

A line appeared between David's brows, and he shifted his stance. "I can wait."

Sam wished he could contact Norma and give her fair warning. Maybe he could track her down at the library. Maybe . . . A familiar figure came into view at the end of the parking area.

Sam's heart rate spiked. Norma was already coming home. There was no way to send David on his way without her noticing him. He exhaled a thready breath. This was it. The moment he hoped would never come. David returning with an apology and a changed heart, begging for forgiveness.

And now, Norma had a decision to make.

David didn't miss Sam's gaze shifting, and he turned, releasing a low whistle when he spotted who was walking their way. Over one shoulder she carried a canvas bag. Likely filled with more books and maybe a few items she'd picked up for dinner. All so ordinary, but not ordinary at all. Not with the situation she was about to walk into.

Sam saw the moment Norma realized who the man was on her doorstep. Her mouth thinned into a line and her brows tugged together. He hoped that was a good sign, that she was displeased, and she'd send her ex away.

"Well hello, darling," David boomed with a grin as she neared.

"David?" Norma looked from him to Sam, then back to him. "What are you doing here?"

"I'm having a nice chat with Sam here," David continued in a voice that was unnecessarily loud. "We're catching up on old times, and he informed me that our little girl's name is Olivia. I love it. Named after your grandmother, right?"

Her cheeks flushed. "Right."

"Norma," Sam said. "Let's go inside. David can be on his way. He has no business here."

"Aw, don't be such a spoilsport, Sam," David said in a mockingly cheerful tone. "I'm the father of that little girl in there. You wouldn't want her to grow up without knowing her real daddy, would you? I can give her a lot more than a shabby student apartment. I'm a partner now in my cousin's shop." The last sentence was directed at Norma.

Sam was done with this man's pretention and snake-oil words. He moved toward David, but was stopped by Norma grasping his arm.

"Sam," she said in a firm tone. "Where's the baby?"

"She's taking a nap."

Norma gave a stiff nod, then turned to face David.

He flashed a smile and held up the flower bouquet he'd

brought. "I only want to talk, Norma. Figure out how all this went wrong between us. Maybe heal a few wounds. There's no reason for us to be strangers. Not when we share a child together."

To her credit, Norma didn't make a move to take the bouquet. "You can't just show up after a year of silence, David, and expect to get anything. I'm married, and Sam's legally adopted Olivia. There's no place for you in our lives."

Something like anger crossed David's face for an instant, but just as quickly, he cleared it. "I understand you're upset about how things ended between us, but I'm here now. I brought you a peace offering and all I want to do is talk. Do you have a few minutes for a man who's come a long way?"

Sam couldn't see Norma's expression, but he could feel her thoughts turning. *Please say no,* he wanted to shout, but he had no right to tell her what to do. Not even as his wife. Because if there was something he wanted more than anything in the world, it was for Norma to choose *him*.

"All right, David," she said. "Let's talk. But then you're leaving."

David's face broke out into a smile. "Of course, of course." He leaned over and set the bouquet of flowers on the lowest step, then straightened. "A walk around the block?"

Norma hesitated, then nodded.

That nod felt like a knife to Sam's chest. She was going to listen to whatever that louse David was going to tell her. But what could Sam do? If he didn't trust his wife, then what was the point? He *needed* to trust her. He *would* trust her.

He slipped the book bag from Norma's shoulder and stepped toward the door. Then he opened it and walked inside. Next, he did one of the hardest things in his life—he shut the door. Resting his forehead against the wood, he released a long breath. For several moments, he just breathed. Then he straightened and moved to the kitchen window that overlooked the parking lot. There . . . Norma and David were walking side by side, David at least a foot taller than she was. Her arms were folded, while he gestured generously with his arms, no doubt creating an elaborate maze of excuses.

How long would they walk together and what would Norma say when she returned? Would she let David see the baby? Would she let him be in Olivia's life? Or even worse, would she forgive her ex and regret her decision to marry Sam?

Was all that he'd done, all that he'd changed and sacrificed for her, about to be swept away and tossed into the trash? Would his love for Norma become insignificant in her eyes?

Yes, he thought, he loved his wife. And he knew she was fond of him. They laughed together, they helped each other, served each other, and were generally compatible. They both doted on Olivia, and if anything took Olivia from him, he didn't know if he'd ever recover from the heartbreak.

The minutes dragged on until a full hour had passed. Now, Sam was pacing. Checking on Olivia, who was apparently having the best nap of her life, then he was pacing again. He stopped at the kitchen window every so often, searching for the pair, but they were long out of sight. Sam shook away any thoughts of them embracing each other, speaking sweet nothings to each other, planning a future . . .

The front door clicked open.

Sam spun to see Norma step inside. Without a word or a glance at him, she shut the door, locked it, then headed to their bedroom. She'd been crying, if her puffy red eyes were any indication.

He remained rooted to the floor, listening as she shut

the bedroom door. The telltale sound of the bedsprings creaking filled the ominous silence. Apparently it wasn't loud enough to awaken the baby. What was Norma doing? Deciding on their future? Coming up with a gentle way to tell Sam she wanted another chance with David?

He sank onto the kitchen chair and dropped his head into his hands. Should he sit here and wait for her to come out? Should he storm into the bedroom and demand answers?

Then he heard a small cry. Olivia was awake.

He wanted to rush to the bedroom and scoop her up—hold her close and kiss her button nose. Smooth her sleep-damp hair from her face and

"Sam?"

He almost didn't hear Norma's whisper. It felt like he was coming out of a deep sleep full of nightmares. Lifting his head, he saw Norma standing in the kitchen entrance, holding Olivia.

He scraped his chair back and stood. "Are you . . . all right?"

Norma's eyes were still red and puffy. She sniffled. "Do you love me, Sam?"

It wasn't even a question he had to think about. It was also something he'd told Norma plenty. But it seemed that in this moment, the question was different than any he'd ever been asked before. And the answer would turn their life either right or left.

"Yes, I love you, Norma," Sam said, his voice cracking. "With all my heart."

She nodded, and new tears slipped down her face. Then she walked toward him and wrapped one arm about him, Olivia nestled between them. He wrapped both of his arms around his girls.

"I love you, too, Sam," Norma whispered.

They'd both said the words before. Many times. But this time her words traveled from her heart to his heart, creating a bond as strong as steel. He tightened his hold and kissed the top of her head.

She released a sigh. "David left. He said he'll be back tomorrow to meet Olivia, but he won't be. I could see it in his eyes."

She drew away and looked up. "I told him I'm in love with you and that our marriage is the best thing that has ever happened to me. I told him that Olivia is your daughter in every way that matters, and if David wants to be in her life, he'll be like an uncle. For once, he took me seriously. For once, he heard the truth. And then he made false promises—ones that a child could see through."

Sam ran his fingers over her cheek. "I'm sorry."

Her eyes glimmered with tears, but her smile appeared. "Don't be sorry. His rejection and cruelty led me to you, and you're the best man in the world, Sam."

His chest expanded with warmth and relief. "In the world, huh?"

She laughed softly. "In my world."

He met her smile with a kiss, reveling in the sweetness that was everything Norma.

"I think we need to celebrate," he said when he drew away.

One of her brows lifted. "Celebrate?"

"Yes, we're celebrating our little family," Sam declared. "We're going out to eat."

Norma's forehead crinkled. "I don't think Olivia's ready for that. She's not going to sit still at a restaurant table."

"We'll take her to the diner," Sam said. "Introduce her to the place it all started. If she can't keep her manners, then we'll box up the food and bring it home. Have a picnic, and she can babble to her heart's content."

Norma's smile widened. "I love you, Sam Davis."

"And I love you, dear Norma."

Nineteen

1981

THE RINGING OF THE PHONE awakened Anita from a dream that fled her mind instantly. She sat up, disoriented, trying to figure out why it was still dark. The clock radio next to her bed said it was only five thirty in the morning. So that's why it was dark, but who was calling?

She scrambled to get out of bed to answer the phone before its ringing awakened Carly.

"Hello?" she said, her voice a scratch.

"Anita," the man said on the other end of the line, "I'm glad I caught you. I know it's early, but—"

Every word of Bobby's was like an ice cube down her back. "Don't you dare cancel on Carly," she broke in.

"Look," he said on a heavy sigh, "I don't have a choice. It's a work thing, but I'll be back in a few days. So I'll call you up and put together another time."

Anita's grip tightened on the receiver. She could try to believe the man, but her knotted stomach told her she'd be lying to herself. "Bobby, if you don't show up tonight, then don't show up at all."

"Hey, that's not fair," he said, his tone defensive. "We're turning over a new leaf, remember? Things happen, and we have to adjust—"

"You're getting back together with Gloria, aren't you?"

"Well... we've been talking."

Anita closed her eyes, hating this, hating everything right now. "One more day," she ground out. "You can delay one more day. Do it for your daughter. Or don't you care at all? Were all those words in the grocery store just platitudes?"

"Anita, I'll be back in a few days. Next week at the latest. I'll call Carly after school. Explain everything. It will be peachy, you'll see."

She wanted to throw something. Anything. She knew by experience that begging, pleading, or even yelling wouldn't change Bobby's mind. "Fine. Whatever." She hung up.

Either he'd call or he wouldn't. There was nothing she could do about it except try to soften the blow for Carly. But first, she needed to get out of the house, out of these four walls, before she combusted.

Anita stepped into the backyard in the predawn light. The moist fragrance of the plants and soil surrounded her, bringing a measure of calm. She walked the dim paths of her garden, letting her disappointment and anger seep out of her. Breathing measured breaths helped to slow her racing heart. As she reached one edge of the garden, she glanced over at Phyllis's house. Strangely, all of her lights were on.

Was that normal for this early in the morning? Anita tried to think of a time when she'd been up this early and outside to notice the lights at Phyllis's. Surely, it had happened, but she had never seen all the lights on. Not even at night.

Her stomach tightened. What if something was wrong? What if there was a medical emergency? Phyllis wasn't a young woman, no matter how healthy she might seem with all of her strict diet fads.

Anita moved toward the gate that led to the front yard. Her steps moved faster until she reached Phyllis's front door. Maybe the lights had been left on from the night before, and she was sound asleep in her bed—oblivious. But from her position, she could see that the bedroom light was on too. Hopefully if she was overreacting, Phyllis would find humor and forgiveness.

Anita knocked on the door, loudly. As she waited for an answer, her heart rate climbed. The phone call from Bobby had been a crappy setback, but it didn't compare to Phyllis having some sort of emergency.

She knocked again and rang the doorbell for good measure. Then she called out, "Phyllis? Are you home?" It was a silly question because her car was nestled beneath the carport. Maybe she'd gone somewhere overnight with her son's family and forgot to turn off the lights?

"Phyllis?" Still there was no answer. Anita couldn't just stand here on the porch, yelling in the near-darkness. "Please be all right," she mumbled as she reached for the doorknob and turned. She fully expected to find it locked, but the door opened.

And that's when she smelled smoke.

"Phyllis!" she yelled, hurrying inside, looking wildly about. Was there a fire, and if so, where was the smoke? She couldn't see anything, but the scent was unmistakable. Her eyes watered as she shouted again.

"Phyllis!"

She hurried into the kitchen to find all the lights on and a scorched pan on the linoleum. None of the stove's elements were on, but whatever had been in the pot was charred beyond recognition.

Anita felt a small measure of relief. There wasn't a fire, it was just a burnt pot. But where was her neighbor?

"Phyllis? Where are you?" she called out as she headed down the hallway.

The bathroom lights were on, but it was empty. The first bedroom lights were on, but Phyllis wasn't in there. It looked like a guest bedroom anyway. The second bedroom lights were on as well.

She stopped in the doorway and gasped. Phyllis was on the bed, curled up on her side, clutching the receiver of her phone. Anita hurried toward her. "Phyllis? What's wrong?"

Phyllis opened her eyes, but said nothing. She seemed to be breathing all right.

"Phyllis, what happened?" she asked, taking the phone receiver.

Phyllis released it easily. Anita put the receiver to her ear. "Hello?" she said in case there was someone on the line. Who had she been trying to call?

Heart thumping, Anita pushed down the switch hook, then dialed 9-1-1. She gave the operator the address, then waited for the ambulance to arrive.

"I've called the ambulance," she told Phyllis as they waited. "Everything will be all right. You'll see." She grasped the woman's hand, holding on, wishing that she knew what had happened.

Her mind raced through scenarios as they waited, and she wondered how to track down Phyllis's son. His name was Cameron, but that's all she really knew.

When the paramedics arrived, Anita answered as many questions as she could. Then she watched as Phyllis was loaded onto a gurney, then into the ambulance. It was an eerie feeling watching her being driven away, leaving her house and neighborhood behind. A few neighbors came out of their houses, and Anita could only tell them the basics.

"Mom?"

Anita heard Carly's voice and turned. She'd come out of the house, wearing a robe, her eyes as wide as saucers. "What's going on?"

Anita hurried over to her. "Phyllis has had a stroke or something. I found her in her house and called the ambulance."

"Will she be okay?" Carly asked in a small voice.

She wrapped her arms about her daughter. "I think so. Her vitals were good, so we just have to wait and see what the doctors say."

Carly nodded against her shoulder. "The ambulance woke me up, and I was worried."

Anita exhaled. "I'm sorry I didn't tell you. Things happened really fast. Come on, I need to find her son's phone number and call him."

They went into Phyllis's house, and Anita rummaged through the kitchen to find an address book. With relief, she found Cameron's number and called it while standing in the middle of Phyllis's kitchen.

Carly sat at the small kitchen table, looking as dazed as Anita felt.

"Cameron," she said when he answered. "This is Anita Gifford, your mother's neighbor. She had a medical incident and was just taken to the hospital."

After the phone call with Cameron, she looked about the kitchen.

"It's weird being here without Phyllis," Carly said.

"It is," she agreed.

"How did you know to come over? Did she call you?"

"No . . ." Anita told Carly about seeing all the lights on, but she didn't bring up the early morning phone call from Bobby yet. "It looks like she burned whatever she was cooking." She picked up the burnt pot from the floor and set it in the sink. "Let's turn off the lights."

Once they'd turned out the lights throughout the house, they headed back home.

"Can we go visit her in the hospital?" Carly asked.

"I think so," Anita said. "Unless they restrict it to family members." She looked over at her daughter and her worried expression. "If you want to skip school today, we can go over in a couple of hours. See if they'll let us visit."

"All right." Carly stepped into the house. "Can we make hot chocolate? I'm not really hungry, but I'm cold."

Anita understood perfectly. Once they had their hot chocolate made, Carly decided to go back to bed.

So Anita found herself alone once again in her kitchen, which felt strange in its familiarity. Perhaps her adrenaline was finally wearing off, but tears started as the house became silent again.

She stood for a long moment, looking out the back windows to the garden that was beginning to come to life with the first hints of dawn. The deep lavender of the sky gradually lightened, promising to be a beautiful day. A day of uncertainty, though, for Phyllis. How was she doing? What had the medical staff discovered?

Anita reached for the phone and settled in a kitchen chair with the phone book. She looked up the hospital number and called, hoping to find out any updates. But the person who answered wouldn't give out any information to a non-family member.

She sighed and hung up the phone. Dropping her head into her hands, she closed her eyes. The argument with Bobby flooded her mind, and she pushed it aside. He could be dealt with later. Phyllis's life was more important.

Anita stood from the table and paced the kitchen, folding her arms against her torso as the kitchen gradually lightened with the sunrise. At least Carly had gone back to sleep, and she could wake her in a couple of hours. She thought through the times when she'd been impatient with her neighbor, and now guilt slammed her in the chest. Phyllis was a sweet woman—nosy, yes, but that was probably a good thing in a neighbor. A neighbor who cared.

Anita moved back to the phone and called another number.

When Wyatt answered, she felt another rise of emotion in her chest. "Hi, Wyatt, I hope I didn't wake you."

"Not exactly," he said. "I just returned from my run." His voice did sound a little breathless.

"Is everything okay, Anita?" he asked.

She realized she hadn't said anything for a moment. "My neighbor Phyllis was just taken to the hospital. You remember her from my backyard?"

"I remember," Wyatt said. "What happened? Will she be all right?"

"I don't know." Anita's voice cracked. She dragged in a breath, then told Wyatt all that had happened.

"It does sound like a stroke or maybe a heart attack," he said. "I'm glad you were able to get ahold of her son."

"Me too." She paused. "I'm happy I didn't wake you."

"I'm glad you called," Wyatt reassured her. "Do you want me to come to the hospital later with you?"

"Oh no, that's fine," she said. "I don't want to take up your day, more than I already have."

His laugh was gentle. "Anita, you can take up my day. There are more important things than meetings and accounts."

She exhaled and closed her eyes. "Thanks for listening."

"Anytime," Wyatt said, "and I mean it."

"I know you do." And she did. She could hear the sincerity in his tone. She could feel it.

The Healing Garden

"So . . . if I'm not going with you to the hospital, can you keep me updated? I'll give you my office phone number."

Anita agreed, and a few minutes later when she hung up with Wyatt, she felt much better. Just sharing what had happened with him made everything feel more manageable. Phyllis was getting the care she needed, and she had aided in that. She had to let herself be relieved and happy about that.

When the phone rang, cutting through the silence, Anita startled. She picked it up, wondering if Wyatt was calling back. Or even Bobby.

"Ms. Gifford?" the man on the other end said. "It's Cameron. I'm at the hospital with my mom, and she told me to call you."

"She's talking?" Relief rushed through her.

"She's talking a little," Cameron said. "She's had a stroke, and the doctors are still running tests to figure out the severity of the damage. She can't move much of her left side right now. Her speech is slow, but understandable."

Anita gripped the receiver tighter. "That's good she can communicate at least."

"Yes," Cameron said, relief in his own tone. "She keeps telling me to tell Anita thank you."

She closed her eyes, the tears starting. "Does she understand what happened?"

"I'm not sure how fully she understands, but she remembers you finding her and calling the ambulance."

Anita nodded to herself. The more time passed, the more of a miracle it seemed that she saw the lights on at Phyllis's house. If Bobby hadn't called . . . not that she wanted to give him any credit, but there it was.

"What do the doctors say about her recovery?" she asked.

"It's too early for answers right now," Cameron said.

"There will definitely be some big changes, though. Probably physical therapy for a while. Maybe a home health nurse. Or we'll bring her to live with us."

Those would all be big changes, indeed.

"Is it okay for me and my daughter to come visit today?"

"I think she'd love that," Cameron said. "I can't thank you enough for finding her and getting her help."

Anita's throat tightened. "I'm grateful it all worked out. She's been a dear neighbor." And it was true, she realized as she thought of Phyllis in a hospital bed, trapped by her body's frailties. The tears were coming back. "Thanks for the update."

After hanging up, Anita rose from the table. The sun had peeked over the horizon finally. With the golden light casting its web over the garden, she headed outside. She'd begin a new canvas this morning. One that she wouldn't ever be paid for, but one that would represent Phyllis. She picked up a basket to collect petals and leaves and began to walk through her garden.

Twenty

ANITA GRASPED CARLY'S HAND AS they approached Phyllis's hospital room. She could hear the murmur of voices coming from inside. Tapping on the partially closed door, she pushed it open to find a blond man with glasses talking to a nurse. They both turned as Anita and Carly hovered in the doorway.

"Cameron?" she said. "I'm Anita."

His expression brightened, and he crossed the room to shake her hand. "Thank you for coming. It's nice to officially meet you."

"You too. This is my daughter, Carly."

Cameron nodded to Carly. "Come on in. She's been asking for you."

He stepped aside, and there was Phyllis, propped up by a few pillows in bed. Her normally immaculate hair was flat, and her eyes were like hollows on her face. But she lifted her right hand.

"Carly . . ." she said slowly. Her expression brightened as Carly moved tentatively toward the bed.

"Hello," Carly said. "I'm sorry you're in the hospital."

"I'm . . . sorry . . . too." Phyllis's mouth lifted on one side. "The . . . food . . . isn't . . . great."

Carly smiled and simultaneously wiped at a tear on her cheek.

Anita moved close and wrapped her arm about her daughter's waist. "It's good to see you, Phyllis. Thanks for letting us visit."

Phyllis reached her hand toward Anita, and she grasped it, holding on tight.

"You . . . found . . . me," she managed to say.

"I did." Anita released a breath. "You had all the lights on in the house, so I decided to check up on you."

Phyllis squeezed her hand. "I . . . don't . . . remember . . . much . . ."

"It's all right," she said. "The important thing is that you're okay, and you'll only get better."

"Cameron . . . came . . ."

"Anita called me, Mother," he said, moving into view on the other side of the bed. "Remember? And of course I came to the hospital."

Tears filled Phyllis's eyes. "He's . . . a . . . good . . . son."

Cameron smiled at her, tears in his own eyes.

Anita's heart expanded. She knew that Phyllis was in good hands with her son. They kept the visit short, and when they left the hospital, her step felt much lighter. She'd watch over the house for her neighbor and stay in touch with Cameron. She and Carly would visit as much as possible and hope for a full recovery.

As they drove back home, Anita finally broke the news to her daughter. "Your father called early this morning. It was actually why I was awake and saw the lights on at Phyllis's house."

Carly looked over at her, knowledge written all over her face. "He's not coming tonight, is he?"

"No." There was no other way to say it. "He said maybe next week."

Carly's shoulders slumped. "Probably not then, either."

The Healing Garden

Anita didn't say anything. She didn't want to confirm that was her belief, too. She didn't want to douse the smallest of hopes.

"Well, I guess his calling to cancel led to one good thing," Carly said quietly.

"Yes, it did." Anita reached over and squeezed her daughter's hand. "Now, what should we do for the rest of your day off?"

"Bake cookies?"

Anita smiled. Who knew such a simple thing with her daughter sounded like the best thing in the world? "It's a deal."

But when they turned onto their street, a red Cadillac sat parked in front of their house.

"Wyatt's here!" Carly said.

Anita's heart beat double time. It looked like the man had just arrived, or was waiting for them. As she pulled into the driveway, he climbed out of his car.

"This is a surprise," she said, wondering if this was a good visit or something to be worried about. It was the middle of the day—had Wyatt come over on a lunch break?

"Sorry I didn't call first," he said. "Well, I did and there wasn't an answer, so I figured you were at the hospital."

"We were," Anita said.

"Phyllis had a stroke," Carly said. "She's talking, though—but it's really slow."

"I'm glad to hear she's speaking. What have the doctors said?"

"We don't have a lot of information yet," Anita said. "They're still doing tests, but her left side is basically immobile. She'll be in the hospital for a few days, then moved to a rehab center for a while."

Wyatt puffed out a breath. "That's rough."

"Her son Cameron is with her, though," Anita continued. "So things are getting taken care of."

"We're going to watch the house," Carly added.

Wyatt smiled. "Of course you are. You're good neighbors to her."

Anita didn't miss the trepidation in his eyes even though his tone was light. "What brings you to our neighborhood in the middle of the day?" she finally asked.

"Oh . . . well, I got a phone call from Lila," he said, slipping his hands into his pockets.

"What?" Carly said. "I thought she said she didn't want to hear from us again."

"That's what I thought too." Wyatt offered a brief smile. "She said that Susan wants to talk to my grandpa. She was very insistent about it, so Lila was finally forced to call me."

"Wow," Anita said. "That's great, right? They can discuss the past and maybe find some healing."

Wyatt gave a short nod. "Yes, right. But here's the thing. Lila told me that Susan wants to talk to Grandpa in person. She won't have it any other way."

"In person?" Carly said. "Is Susan coming to visit, then?"

"Not exactly." Wyatt rotated his shoulders. "Lila said that Susan doesn't travel. So I'm going to have to take Gramps to her."

Anita stared at him. "Will your grandpa be up for the road trip?"

"I honestly don't know," he said. "I need to talk to the medical director at the center. Find out if he's under any traveling restrictions. I don't think he is, though. I'd just have to be updated on his medication schedule and his general routine."

Anita watched the worry flit across his face. "That's a lot of responsibility to take him by yourself."

The Healing Garden

"Yeah, I thought so too," Wyatt continued. "I talked to my sister about an hour ago, and there's no way she can get any days off work right now. She just took a vacation last month."

Anita didn't know if he was asking, directly or indirectly, but he had driven to her house in the middle of the day to talk about this. "When are you thinking of going?"

"This weekend, if possible." Wyatt folded his arms. "I mean, waiting only drags everything out."

"How long of a trip?"

Wyatt's gaze focused on her—he knew where this was leading. "Three days. Driving one day, the second day for the visit, then returning the third."

"Carly and I can come with you if you want extra help."

Carly squealed. "Really, Mom?"

"Really," she said, but kept her gaze on Wyatt.

His expression was one of gratitude and relief. "Are you sure? I mean, I wouldn't ask if it weren't important, because I know you have your own lives."

She touched his arm. "I'm sure. It will be a fun adventure, and as you can see, Carly is ready to pack."

Carly laughed and hugged Anita, then she hugged Wyatt.

He gave a surprised laugh and patted her back. "I still have to get clearance from the center, but it's a go if we do."

"Well, call them right now," Carly said. "We have a phone, you know."

"Carly . . ." Anita said in a warning tone.

But she just grinned and ran toward the house. "I'm going to look for the suitcase."

Anita set her hands on her hips as she watched her daughter go. "This trip might be more than you're bargaining for."

"I'll take that chance," Wyatt said, his eyes smiling. "I think I will call right now if you don't mind me borrowing your phone."

"I don't mind."

Twenty minutes later, they had the beginnings of a road trip plan in place. Wyatt had received permission from the center to pack up his grandfather, and of course Mr. Davis was on board. Now, Anita just had to make lists of the to-dos to get ready for the trip. Carly had her bedroom in disarray as she tried to decide what to pack.

"It's only two nights," Anita told her when she came out of her bedroom for the tenth time to ask a question, Sassy trailing behind her.

Anita and Wyatt were sitting at the kitchen table, writing down details.

"Will there be a pool at the hotel?" Carly asked, looking between the two of them.

"I don't know because Wyatt hasn't called to book one yet."

"I'll get on that as soon as possible," he said with a chuckle.

Carly scrunched her face, then disappeared back into her bedroom.

"Sorry." Anita winced. "She's excited, to say the least. It's a good distraction for her, though, after the disappointment from her dad."

Wyatt's brows furrowed. "What disappointment?"

"Oh, uh . . ." Anita exhaled. "This morning Bobby called early and canceled. Said he was leaving town for work, but . . . I think that's just an excuse."

Wyatt's jaw clenched. "He couldn't wait one more day?"

"That's what I asked." Anita lifted a shoulder. "I can't control his actions, and I'll go crazy if I try. Carly is actually doing pretty okay with it. Better than me."

Wyatt covered her hand with his own. "I'm sorry he did that to you, to the both of you. He's missing out on a great kid."

Tears pricked, and Anita blinked them away. "Thanks, Wyatt," she said in a quiet voice. "You showing up here today of all days was kind of fortuitous."

He tightened his hold on her hand, and she appreciated the touch, the connection. "I'm glad everything is coming together, then."

She nodded, but didn't say anything.

"She'll be all right, Anita," Wyatt continued. "Carly's a great girl who has an amazing mom. You've been there for her through everything, and you need to be kinder to yourself."

"To myself?"

"Yeah, you're too hard on yourself," Wyatt said, his thumb tracing over her hand. "From where I'm sitting, you've provided your daughter a safe and loving home. She's talented, intelligent, and has a good heart. Just like her mom."

She stared at him for a moment.

"It's okay to accept a compliment," he said, the edge of his mouth lifting. "Just say thank you."

Anita smiled. "Thank you." Then she leaned forward and hugged him. It was just a hug—a friendship hug—but something deep inside of her wished it were more.

"Meow," Sassy interrupted.

Anita drew away from Wyatt, grateful but also disappointed in the interruption. She could focus on the cat without him seeing how much she was probably blushing. "Are you hungry, Sassy?"

She answered with another meow, and Anita rose from the table and crossed to the pantry to get the cat food.

"I should probably get going," Wyatt said, standing too. "I need to go to the office for a couple of hours and reschedule some things. Book a hotel. See if I need to pick anything up for my grandpa for the trip. Do you need anything else?"

Anita looked over at him. His steady green gaze made things inside of her melt. The atmosphere in the room had changed. His holding her hand, then his kind words, and then their shared hug . . . Was she doing the right thing by agreeing to this road trip? It went beyond casual friendship. It was involving her daughter, and it was involving both of their hearts.

"I don't think so," she said. "If I need something, I can run to the store. I'm just going to talk with one of the neighbors about feeding Sassy. Usually Phyllis does it when we go out of town."

Wyatt nodded, his gaze still on her. "Okay. Call me if you need my help. I'll be doing errands tonight and can get whatever you need." He moved a couple of steps closer. "Thanks again for coming. It means a lot to me."

Anita's throat felt dry, and her cheeks warmed again. "You're welcome," she managed to say.

Then Wyatt moved another step closer and kissed her cheek. "See you tomorrow morning."

He stepped away, and before she could figure out what her reaction should be, he headed out of the kitchen.

She remained in her spot by the pantry as she listened to the front door open, then close. Moments later, she heard the sound of his car engine start.

Anita touched her cheek where Wyatt had kissed her. Was this happening? It was happening. What did she think about it? What was she feeling? Her heart was racing, her pulse was pounding, and she was . . . smiling. She wanted to run outside and demand a real kiss. She also wanted to run

The Healing Garden

to her bedroom and burrow under the covers until the sun came up again.

"You're blushing," Carly said in a matter-of-fact tone.

Anita flinched. "Oh, I didn't hear you."

Carly smirked. "You like him, Mom. You might as well admit it."

"Like who?"

Carly tugged open the refrigerator door and pulled out the pitcher of orange juice. "It's okay," she said nonchalantly. "I like him too, and it's all right with me if you want to date him."

Anita opened her mouth, then shut it as she watched her daughter walk down the hallway, carrying her cup of juice with her. Apparently, Carly was getting the last word.

Twenty-one

"Where's Mr. Davis?" Carly asked as they loaded their bags into the trunk of the Cadillac.

"When I stopped by, he wasn't quite ready," Wyatt said. "I thought I'd come here and pick you up, then we can go back to the center. I guess he had a rough night."

Anita's gaze connected with his over the hood of the car. "Is everything all right?"

"They assured me it was," he said, but she didn't miss the concern etched on his face.

They slid into the seats and Wyatt started the engine. "I guess he woke up from a nightmare, and after they got him settled, he couldn't fall back asleep for a couple of hours."

"Well, I can always take another day off from school if we need to delay the trip," Carly said in a nonchalant tone.

"Let's hope that doesn't need to happen," Wyatt said, backing the car out. They pulled onto the road. "Everything's set up with Susan and Lila, and all the other arrangements. It would be a shame to cancel it."

"Everything will be fine, you'll see," Anita said, hoping it would be the case. She patted Wyatt's hand, and he glanced over at her with a smile.

Her heart did a little tumble.

Carly put on her headphones and pressed Play on whatever cassette she'd put into her Walkman.

The Healing Garden

"I talked to Phyllis's son this morning," Anita said. "He's staying at her house."

"Ah, how's Phyllis?" Wyatt asked.

"She'll probably be moved today or tomorrow to the rehab facility. He's going to feed our cat while we're gone. Said it was the least he could do to thank me for finding her."

Wyatt smiled. "Good plan." He paused. "You didn't call last night. Do you have everything you need?"

"I think so . . ." Anita glanced at Carly in the back seat. Her head was bobbing to whatever music she was listening to as she looked out the side window. "Um, Carly has noticed our, uh . . . interactions."

Wyatt raised a brow. "Like when I kissed your cheek?"

"Not that," Anita said, warmth shooting through her. "Other things . . . I don't know exactly, but she accused me of liking you."

Wyatt didn't answer for a moment. After turning the next corner, he asked, "*Do* you like me?"

He said it so softly, so tenderly, that Anita didn't feel as embarrassed as she might. "I like you, Wyatt, but I don't really know what that means."

He gave a short nod. "Is Carly upset that you might like me?"

"No, quite the opposite in fact."

Wyatt's smile appeared. "Like I said before, Carly's a smart kid."

Anita laughed, then stifled it to avoid drawing her daughter's attention to the front seat.

"Anita," Wyatt said in a low voice. "I like you too. And I don't know what it means either. I like being around you, and I like everything I know about you so far."

"I'm good at hiding my flaws," she said.

"Hmm." He reached for her hand and threaded their fingers.

From Carly's position, she wouldn't be able to see the hand holding, but it felt risqué all the same.

Wyatt's hand was warm, his fingers long, his grasp firm. Their hands fit well together, and Anita wondered if she'd ever had so many goose bumps racing up her arm when it wasn't cold.

"My life is complicated," she said quietly.

Wyatt glanced over at her, his green eyes intense. "And you handle the complications with grace, which is another thing I like about you."

"My head it getting pretty big by now."

"As it should." He moved his thumb slowly over her skin.

All too soon, they arrived at the center, and he released her hand. Which was a good thing because the longer he held it, the more she wanted from him. And she hadn't been glib when she told Wyatt her life was complicated. Dating a man didn't just involve her, it would involve Carly. And her last choice—Glenn—had proved to Anita that she didn't always make the best choices. She didn't want that to become a pattern.

"He's ready!" Carly announced from the back seat, in a too-loud voice. She tugged off her headphones.

"Inside voice," Anita said with a laugh.

"Sorry," she said, not sounding sorry at all.

Sure enough, Mr. Davis sat in a wheelchair, situated in front of the glass doors of the center. A small suitcase stood off to one side, and a nurse was fussing with getting a sweater on him.

"Looks like he's pretty anxious to get going," Wyatt said, both humor and relief in his voice.

"Our road trip is back on," Anita added.

They all climbed out of the car and greeted Mr. Davis. He beamed at them. "Ready for our adventure?"

The Healing Garden

"We're ready, Gramps," Wyatt said. "How are you feeling?"

"Oh, I'm fine. The nurses here are just fussy." He smiled over at Ginny, who shook her head good-naturedly. "See, I have an entire army to help me."

"That you do, Mr. Davis," Ginny said, squeezing his shoulder. "Now, let's get you settled."

"Are we taking the wheelchair?" Wyatt asked.

"No," his grandpa said. "This is just for show—giving me the five-star treatment to get into my own car. I told them I'll do just fine with my regular old walker."

When Wyatt opened the passenger side door, Mr. Davis said, "Oh no, I'll sit in the back with Carly."

"I'm all right in the back," Anita protested. "We want to make sure you're comfortable."

But Mr. Davis waved her off. "I've already made up my mind. You're up front."

She glanced at Wyatt, and he shrugged. "All right," she conceded.

Once Mr. Davis was settled into the back seat with a lap blanket that he claimed he didn't need, Anita climbed into the front seat. She was both excited and nervous about this trip. Excited to find out the full story about Susan and Mr. Davis, but nervous about it bringing up previous sadness and regret.

"How long is this drive?" he said as they pulled out of the parking lot.

"Eight or nine hours at least," Wyatt said. "We have some planned stops on the way."

"That sounds fine. Did you give Susan and her daughter a time when we'd arrive?"

"Yes, they're expecting us for a brunch tomorrow," Wyatt said. "We'll stop at a grocery store so we can contribute a few items. Lila thought a brunch would be best in case we need to sleep in."

Anita glanced back at Mr. Davis when Carly asked, "Are you nervous?"

"I'm as nervous as a turkey in November," he said, but his eyes twinkled. "I'm happy her daughter is allowing the visit. I hate to think about Susan being upset with me."

Carly reached over and patted his hand. "It's probably just a misunderstanding."

"How old are you?" he asked.

She grinned. "Teenagers are more mature these days than back in your time."

He chuckled. "Maybe, and smarter too. You have all those newfangled gadgets to figure out."

"Like this?" Carly held up her Walkman. "It's great when Mom wants to listen to the news, and I want to listen to my music. Do you want to try it?"

And the conversation between the pair of them continued. Anita's heart soared at their friendship. Since her own parents were long gone, Carly didn't have grandparents she saw.

Wyatt glanced over at her. "Everything okay?" he asked in a quiet voice.

"Yeah, I love their banter."

"Me too." He smiled and reached for her hand.

Wyatt holding her hand felt strange and wonderful at the same time. Anita could get used to this. Expanding her relationships, living richer moments, going on interesting quests into the past.

"Speaking of news," Mr. Davis said in a louder voice from the back seat. "How about we put the radio on? I've been living in a land of three square meals and board games. I don't know what's going on in the outside world."

The Healing Garden

So Wyatt put the radio on a news station, and for the next part of their journey, the news updates blared through. At one point, Carly tapped Anita on her shoulder. She looked back to see that Mr. Davis had fallen asleep, his head resting on Carly's shoulder.

Carly smiled, and Anita reached over to turn down the radio volume. "Your grandpa is asleep," she told Wyatt.

He looked in the rearview mirror. "I think we'll continue past this next town, and when he wakes up, we can stop for lunch."

"Will that take you off your plan too much?"

"We're making good time," he said. "Besides, part of the fun is getting to drive this more than about the town."

Anita ran her hand over the smooth leather upholstery. "No complaints here."

Within the next few minutes, Carly had closed her eyes too, her headphones on.

"If you're tired, you can sleep," Wyatt said in a teasing tone.

"Then who'll watch the road for you?"

"Ha. Right. I do need you awake."

He squeezed her hand because he was currently holding it. It was a soaring feeling to be holding hands with this man—a man she hadn't even kissed yet. She hoped that would change, and fairly soon, but for now, she could wait.

The hours passed by surprisingly quickly, and when they pulled up to the hotel Wyatt had booked, Anita should have been tired. But she wasn't. They ate a simple meal at a nearby restaurant, then split up to their rooms, Wyatt and his grandpa in one room, and Anita and Carly sharing another.

"Are you going to be able to sleep, Sam?" Carly asked Mr. Davis.

It felt a bit odd to hear her daughter call him by his first name, but he kept insisting that they both call him Sam.

"I'll be sleeping fine," Sam said. "I just need to be sure to fall asleep first so that Wyatt's snoring doesn't keep me awake."

"Hey, I don't snore," he protested. Then he mouthed to Anita, "It's true."

She laughed. "In the morning, you can tell us who snored."

"Huh," Sam said, then he threw a smile at Carly. "I hope you sleep well. You'll need to be on your toes tomorrow. History is about to be made."

Once they were settled in their rooms, Carly turned to face Anita from her bed. "Do you think that Sam would change his past if he could? About Susan?"

"I don't think so," she said. "He seems devoted to Norma, and Wyatt has come to the same conclusion. Although I think he was a bit worried for a while."

Carly stifled a yawn. "What do you think the big misunderstanding was?"

"Oh . . ." Anita's mind whirled. "I can't guess, but I do know that there are a lot of misunderstandings in a couple's relationship. And if the other person doesn't voice their concern, then it will never be discussed. Could cause resentment."

"Which is probably what happened." Carly turned onto her back and folded her hands behind her head. "I can't wait to meet Susan. Even though she and Sam are both old now, it's kind of sweet to think about them being in love in high school."

Anita smiled at that. "I agree." She reached over to turn off the lamp. "See you in the morning, sweetie."

"Good night, Mom."

Twenty-two

It turned out that Anita was the one who didn't sleep much. She lay awake until at least midnight, then seemed to stir every hour.

"Sleep well?" Wyatt asked when she covered her mouth to stifle a second yawn as they walked to the car the following morning.

"Oh, sorry," she said with a sheepish smile. "I feel like I was awake all night. Have you ever had that happen?"

"Sure," he said. "Good thing I'm driving."

"Yeah, and thanks for that. I'll have to get something caffeinated later on." Anita decided she liked Wyatt first thing in the morning. He wasn't overly peppy, or dragging either; he was just himself. Oh, and he looked good in a pair of 501s and a polo shirt.

"Well, if you need a nap after our meeting with Susan, we can take a break."

"I'll let you know."

"I slept like a baby," Sam announced, his walker's wheels clattering on the asphalt as they walked. "Like a baby with a full stomach, enjoying happy dreams."

Carly laughed. "Babies usually wake up crying in the middle of the night. Why is 'sleeping like a baby' even a saying?"

"I think it's because babies can sleep through a lot of

noise," he said. "At least when they're young. I remember Wyatt's mother—she could sleep through anything. Unless she didn't want to. Wyatt, on the other hand, would wake at the smallest of sounds."

Wyatt helped his grandpa into the car, then shut the door. He turned to Anita. "Don't believe everything he says."

She smiled. "Are you a light sleeper?"

"I can be." He shrugged. "Last night I think I slept a lot better than you."

Anita was battling another yawn. "How can you tell?"

Wyatt smirked, then squeezed her hand and moved around to the other side of the car.

"Here we go," Sam announced to the car at large. "We're about to meet my first love." He cleared his throat. "Be it known to everyone that I loved my wife Norma more than life itself."

"Thanks, Gramps," Wyatt said.

"I was wondering about that," Carly said brightly. "Can you love two women in a lifetime?"

"I think so, but for me, it was two different loves," Sam said. "With Susan, I loved her and our hope for the future. With Norma, I loved her and our life together—which was my present, then became my future. When you live and work and sacrifice with another person, your love deepens to a level that's hard to explain. I think with Susan, my affection for her was more in what-ifs."

"That's really deep, Sam," Carly said.

He grinned, and Wyatt laughed. "It is really deep, but probably accurate."

"Wyatt, here, loved a woman," Sam said, patting his shoulder. "The love wasn't deep enough to last, though."

Wyatt glanced at Anita. "Uh, thanks, Gramps. That's true too."

She only smiled, then she took his hand.

"Is that how it was with Dad?" Carly asked her.

"Oh." A spark of panic rushed through her. "I think your dad and I had different opinions of what marriage meant. We definitely loved each other, but we were interested in different futures."

"I guess love and relationships are a lot more than just feelings? They're actions too," Carly said.

"I think you're the smartest teenager I know," Sam said.

"And maybe the only one you know?" She laughed.

Wyatt slowed the car and stopped at the curb of a small house with white shutters and planters filled with flowers on the front porch. "This must be it."

"It's cute," Carly said.

He turned off the engine and looked back at his grandpa, who was staring out the car window.

After a long moment of silence, Sam said, "I'm ready."

Wyatt climbed out of the car and opened his door to help him out. Anita grabbed the folded-up walker and handed it over.

With a trembling hand, Sam grasped the handles. He didn't protest when Wyatt held on to his other arm as they walked toward the house. Carly and Anita followed, and she had to tell herself to breathe.

Once they were all on the porch, Wyatt rang the doorbell, and then they waited.

Any moment now . . . The door finally creaked open, and there stood a woman who had to be Susan's daughter. Anita guessed the blonde woman to be around fifty years old, with some silver threaded through her short hairstyle.

"Lila?" Wyatt asked. "I'm Wyatt Davis, and this is my grandfather Sam."

Lila's mouth was set in a firm line, but her light blue

eyes were plenty curious. Her gaze took in the four visitors, then she opened the door wider.

"I'm Anita," Anita offered, "and this is my daughter Carly."

Lila nodded. "Wyatt said you'd all be coming." She stepped back. "Well, come on in. My mother's been talking nonstop about Sam, so we might as well get this meeting started."

"Hang on to me, Wyatt," he said. "I'll leave the walker out here."

They went into the house. Anita glanced around, wondering where Susan was. The woman wasn't in sight, though. The interior was mostly blues and pinks, likely the favorite color of one of the women in the house.

"This way," Lila said. "We're set up on the back patio. Mother likes to watch the birds and butterflies. She'll stay out there all day if I let her."

They continued through the kitchen, where a couple of Crock Pots were steaming away. They smelled delicious. But at this moment, Anita didn't think she could eat a thing. Not when her stomach was in knots of anticipation.

Lila stepped onto the back patio first, followed by Wyatt and Sam.

A round table had been set with bowls, glasses, and utensils. In the middle of the table was a flower arrangement that nearly blocked the view of a petite elderly lady sitting in a chair. The woman's hair was a snowy white, but her blue eyes were as bright as her daughter's. It was clear she'd put some effort into her appearance, since her lips and cheeks were a soft pink.

Her expression looked as if it were caught between a smile and surprise.

"Susan," Sam said, the word more like a question.

She set a liver-spotted hand on the table's edge and pushed up to a standing position. "Sam, is that you?"

Sam broke away from Wyatt's grasp and moved around the table toward her. He reached out a hand, and Susan grasped it, hers trembling and his more steady.

"I can't believe you look the same," she said.

Sam chuckled. "I've changed quite a bit. It's you who looks the same."

Susan's cheeks flushed, and she touched her white hair. "This has changed."

He lifted his gaze to her hair. "I always knew you were a blonde."

Susan tightened her hold on his hand because they were still clasped. "You always teased me. I see that hasn't changed."

He shook his head slowly. "I got your postcard."

"I was hoping you would," Susan said. "I waited, you know, until the obituary came out."

"Norma's?" Surprise was clear in his tone.

She nodded, and then her eyes filled with tears.

"Oh, Susan . . ."

Still holding her hand, Sam guided her to sit back down, and he settled into the chair next to her. It was like no one else was around, and they were having a private conversation.

"I know I shouldn't have been pining all these years," she said, taking a napkin from the table and dabbing at her eyes. "I tried to move on and let you go. I really did."

Sam's forehead creased into a frown. "I thought you were in love and that you were happy to marry your sweetheart. Your announcement was the last letter I ever received from you." He drew in a breath. "I kept writing, you know, just to wish you all the best and to ask for any updates.

No more letters came, though. And once I married Norma, I decided that was that."

She nodded, looking down at their clasped hands. "I was too late . . . I waited too long . . ."

"What are you talking about?" Sam asked. "What were you too late for?"

Suddenly, Susan seemed to notice they weren't alone and had a rather captive audience. She looked across the table. "Who do we have here?"

Wyatt cleared his throat. "My name is Wyatt, and I'm Sam's grandson. These are our friends, Anita and her daughter Carly."

"Welcome," Susan said with a gracious smile, as if she hadn't just been tearful. "Make yourselves at home and have a seat. Lila can bring in the soups. We know you've had a long drive."

"Oh, I can help Lila," Anita said immediately, although she kind of wanted to stay and hear any conversation between Susan and Sam.

Lila waved her off, though. "You stay and hear what Susan has to say. Maybe you can help with cleanup."

She hesitated. "If you're sure."

Lila gave her a brief smile, then nodded. "Of course I'm sure, or I wouldn't have suggested it." She hurried away before Anita could reply.

Wyatt held out a chair for her to sit down. Carly had already helped herself to the seat on the other side of Sam.

Susan watched them with bright eyes. "Are you married? Dating?"

"Us?" Anita said. "No, we're friends. That's all."

Wyatt nudged her knee with his knee. She nudged him back. "We are friends, but that's not all," he said.

Anita gaped at him, but Susan just continued to smile.

The Healing Garden

"Young love is wonderful." She released a wistful sigh, then reached for the glass at her place setting.

"Let me fill that for you," Sam said, when she realized it was empty. He reached for the pitcher of ice water and filled her glass.

"Thank you, Sam," she said, taking a sip, then setting the glass down. "Now, tell me about your children and grandchildren."

Sam blinked as if he were trying to clear his thoughts. "Wyatt and his sister Paula are what's left of my posterity."

"Oh, I thought you had more . . ." Her voice trailed off.

"No," Sam said. "Norma couldn't have any more children after our daughter was born."

Susan gave a slow nod. "I'm sorry to hear that. The town was gossipy about that when I returned. Said you had to get married on account of knocking her up." She laughed, her cheeks flushed. "But knowing what kind of man you were, I was not surprised. You'd never run from your mistakes."

"It wasn't a mistake," Sam said in a quiet voice, but it resonated across the patio.

Lila stepped outside just then, carrying two bowls of steaming soup.

Wyatt moved to his feet to take them from her. Lila didn't return inside, though. Instead, she remained to listen.

"I didn't mean that, Sam," Susan corrected. "I just meant the gossip—"

He lifted a hand. "The gossips didn't know anything." He cast a glance at Wyatt. "Norma became pregnant by another man—her boyfriend at the time. He ditched her, and well . . . I married her and adopted her daughter."

Anita was pretty sure this was new information to not only Susan, but to Wyatt himself. His whole body stilled as he stared at his grandpa.

"Gramps?" he said in a strained voice. "What are you talking about?"

Sam turned his head to look at him. "I married your grandmother so that her child would be legitimate. I cared for Norma very much, and over the months and years, I grew to love her deeply."

Wyatt rubbed at his jaw. "You're not . . . my grandfather by blood?"

Sam shook his head slowly, then reached for Wyatt's arm. "Your mother was my daughter in every other way possible. Her biological father tried to visit once when she was a few months old, then disappeared again. He never actually saw her in person."

Wyatt exhaled. "That's a pretty major thing to keep from me my entire life."

"I understand how you might think that, but in my generation, we kept things private."

Wyatt closed his eyes for a moment, and Anita grasped his hand.

"You married Norma to save her reputation?" Susan said, her voice incredulous.

Sam turned his attention back to her. "Norma and I were good friends, and you had already written me about your engagement. It didn't cross my mind that I wasn't doing the right thing by moving forward with my life."

Susan reached a trembling hand for her glass of water. After another sip, she said, "I came back, Sam. I saw the two of you in that old diner. You were sitting close to her on the same side of the booth, your arm around her. She laughed at something you said, and then you kissed her." She drew in a breath. "I left after seeing you together, and that's when I heard the two of you were engaged."

"I didn't know you came back," Sam said. He was the one surprised now. "Why didn't you tell me?"

Susan shrugged, and tears filled her eyes. "I guess I wanted to surprise you. I broke off the engagement, and I wrote to you about it. You never replied. A few weeks later, I decided to throw all caution to the wind and return. It had been so long anyway, and I wanted closure, I guess. But I also hoped that maybe things between us could work out after all."

Sam's shoulders sagged.

"But now I realize, even if I had walked into the diner that night . . . you still would have chosen Norma."

The conflict in his gaze wrenched at Anita's emotions. This was all so much . . . and she could only imagine what Wyatt was feeling with such a shocking revelation.

"Susan . . ." Sam began, his voice cracking with emotion. "I never received that letter about your canceled engagement." He released a shuddering breath. "And I can't say what decision I might have made if I had received the letter, but if there's anything I've learned in more than eighty years of living, it's that the past can't be changed. We can only move forward."

Susan dabbed at a fresh round of tears. "You never received my letter?"

"No, and I don't understand why not."

She heaved. "My father was furious that I canceled the engagement. Now I wonder . . . if he never posted my letters to you. I'd leave them in the basket of outgoing mail."

Sam and Susan were both quiet for a long moment. Anita was pretty sure the soup Lila had brought out was cold now, but no one seemed to care.

"What did you do after you left Seattle?" Sam finally asked in a quiet voice.

"I went back home and faced the wrath of my father," Susan said. "I'd spent all my savings on that trip—it was meant to go toward my wedding." She gave a little shrug. "A few months later, Clyde started coming around again, and we ended up getting married."

Lila headed back into the house.

"And your kids and grandkids?" Sam prodded gently.

"Two children," she said. "Lila and Clyde Jr. The marriage wasn't . . . great." She cast a furtive look toward the house, where Lila had disappeared. "Clyde enjoyed his drinking. He died at fifty-four, and I was widowed. No interest in remarrying after that."

"I'm sorry for your pain," Sam said.

"I went back to Seattle for a few weeks about ten years ago," Susan said. "I visited all the old haunts, looked up some former friends, but never had the courage to knock on your door. I figured you didn't want to see a ghost from the past. I even heard about Norma's health problems, and I selfishly checked obituaries from time to time."

Sam didn't act shocked or bothered. "I suppose curiosity can get the best of us."

She nodded, her smile faint. "Norma was a lucky woman, and I . . . I could have done things differently. I could have returned to Seattle much sooner. Or made an effort to meet you somehow after the Spanish flu danger was over. I could have turned down Clyde. I wouldn't have wanted to miss out on my children, though. They've been my comfort through everything."

Lila was back with more bowls of soup, this time balancing them on a tray.

Wyatt moved to his feet to help.

"Lunch is served," she said softly.

Anita wondered how much Lila had known about all of this—at least on her mother's side. Now, she knew Sam's side.

"Children, however they come, are always a blessing," he said.

"Amen," Carly said. "Now can we eat? I'm starving."

Anita stifled a laugh—she couldn't help it. Apparently Carly hadn't been entranced like everyone else.

"Help yourself," Susan said. "All this emotional stuff has made me ravenous."

Sam gave her a tender smile, then the two of them began to eat the soup.

Twenty-three

"THIS WAS MY MOTHER'S RECIPE," Susan told Carly as a gentle breeze brought the fragrance of flowers from the yard. "I thought Sam would appreciate something from our childhood."

"I think he does," Carly told the older woman. They both glanced over at Sam and Lila, who were taking a tour of the garden.

"I used to garden," Susan said on a sigh. "Lila's taken over now, and she does an excellent job. I miss it, but my bones aren't what they used to be."

"My mom uses her garden in her art," Carly said.

"Oh?" Susan turned her bright gaze upon Anita.

"I do, in fact." She explained her artwork and process, and Susan seemed fascinated.

"I'd love to see your work," she said, then her brow furrowed. "Or maybe you can send me a photo?"

"I could do that," Anita said. "Can you travel at all?"

"Not for a long time now . . ." Susan's voice trailed off, and her attention redirected to where Sam stood with Lila. They seemed to be in deep conversation about something.

Wyatt came out of the house, where he'd insisted on doing all the cleanup so the others could visit. His gaze held Anita's for a second as if to silently ask her if things were going all right. She nodded. She'd guessed he needed some time alone to process all that his grandpa had said about his mother not being biologically related to him.

Wyatt moved past the table and walked into the yard on the opposite side of where Sam and Lila stood.

Since Carly seemed perfectly content to chat with Susan, Anita rose and followed Wyatt. She stopped near him where he stood by a fruit tree.

"Are you all right?" she asked in a soft voice. "Your grandpa's news was a lot to take in."

Wyatt nodded, then sighed. "I don't know why it was kept secret. Maybe in their era that was how things were done, but waiting this long? How do I tell my sister?"

"Do you think she'll be upset?"

"No idea. Shocked, of course."

It might be a bold move, but Anita wrapped her arms about his waist. Wyatt didn't hesitate, pulling her into a tight hug.

"I'm sorry for all the hard things going on," she said.

He rested his chin atop her head. "Thanks for commiserating. I think it's good to get everything out. To get the truth spoken. I can tell Susan has suffered because of the misunderstandings."

Anita drew away and dropped her arms. "Maybe this trip will give them both the peace they're looking for."

Wyatt's eyes were steady on hers. "I believe it will." He glanced over at his grandpa. "I don't know where everything will go from here—if they'll stay in touch—but I'm glad we came this weekend." His gaze returned to Anita. "And I'm glad you came with me."

She lifted a shoulder. "It's been great for Carly. She's made a new best friend."

Wyatt chuckled. "Looks like it." He reached for her hand and rubbed his thumb over her skin.

Anita could stay in this spot all day, among the fragrant trees, holding Wyatt's hand. She could also kiss this man, but now wasn't the time or the place. Every argument she thought up about dating him quickly died. Carly enjoyed him, and well, Anita enjoyed him too. He'd received a hard blow today, but was handling it with grace. He was attentive and interested in her life. He wasn't put off by a teenager and seemed to genuinely like Carly. And he wanted what was best for his grandpa.

"Looks like Gramps is taking his spot again next to Susan," Wyatt said.

She looked over at the patio. Sam settled into the chair next to her and they leaned toward each other. "I can almost imagine them as teenagers."

Carly laughed at something Lila said.

"Maybe we're missing out on all the fun," Wyatt said.

She nudged him. "I'm kind of having fun right here."

He squeezed her hand. "Me too."

They spent another hour at Susan's home, and by the time they headed back to the hotel, Anita could tell Sam was exhausted.

Wyatt aided him out of the car and into the hotel lobby, and they all shuffled along the hall to their rooms.

"What are you going to do now, Sam?" Carly asked. "Visit each other once a month?"

He chuckled. "We're going to be pen pals. And maybe have a few phone conversations. But I think we both know that we have our separate lives. Have had for a long time."

Carly frowned. "But she came back for you."

"She did," Sam said. "And as sweet and hopeful as that gesture was, I think she was just running from her decision about Clyde. She couldn't bring herself to not marry him unless she had some grand excuse. She was going to use me as her escape, not because . . ."

When his voice trailed off, Carly asked, "Because what?"

"Not because she was in love with me the same way I'd been in love with her." He patted Carly's arm. "Love is very complicated. And I know, or at least I hope I know, that I would have still chosen Norma. My relationship with Susan was important and full of light when we were together. But we let too many years and decisions come between us—too many times we chose other things over each other. I discovered in my marriage that choosing each other should always come first." He paused. "I didn't have that with Susan."

Carly smiled, although it was a bit of a sad smile. "She's a nice lady."

"She is," Sam agreed.

When they reached their hotel rooms across from each other, Carly asked, "Does anyone want to go swimming?"

"I'll let you youngsters enjoy the pool," Sam said. "You should go with them, Wyatt. No use sitting in the hotel room listening to me sleep." He winked at Carly.

"All right," he said. "I'll meet you at the pool in a little bit."

Carly grinned and turned to their door to unlock it.

"See you soon," Anita told the men.

Once inside their room, she found her daughter sitting on the edge of her bed, hands folded in her lap. "Did you change your mind about swimming?"

"No . . ." Carly sighed. "It's kind of sad to know that there's not going to be a romance between Sam and Susan."

Anita gave a short laugh. "What? Was that what you were hoping for?"

"Of course." Carly folded her arms. "But all the stuff he said seemed right. Is that how it was with you and Dad? You didn't choose each other, so things fell apart?"

Anita should have expected this question after hearing what Sam had said. "I think Mr. Davis is a wise man, and although we can't compare relationships to each other, his words hold a lot of truth."

She seemed to think about this. "I want to call Dad. Do you have his number?"

Anita did, but she was surprised that Carly didn't have it. "I'll write it down," she said, picking up the hotel notepad. She wrote the number and handed it over.

"I know it's long distance," Carly said. "But it will be a short phone call."

"Take whatever time you need." Anita moved toward the door. "Do you want me to give you some privacy?"

"Okay."

She stepped out of the room. She decided this was a good thing on Carly's part, but that didn't make her any less nervous about her daughter having her feelings hurt . . . again.

After about ten minutes, the door on the other side of the hallway opened. Wyatt came out, wearing a swimsuit. He had a towel draped over one shoulder. Anita tried not to check him out too much—it was rude, right? But she couldn't help but notice that all his running had helped in the physique department. She wasn't one to ogle a man like some of her high school friends did back in the day, but that didn't mean she couldn't appreciate Wyatt.

"Oh hi," he said. "Are you . . . locked out?"

"No." She felt her skin heat, and she tried to keep her focus on his face. "Carly's speaking to Bobby, so I'm giving her some privacy."

"Oh." His brow furrowed, and she loved that he was concerned with the news. "Everything okay?"

"I think so." Anita shrugged. "Your grandpa's experience brought up some questions, I guess."

Wyatt moved to her side of the hallway. "I think I was surprised—I mean, I wondered if this reunion would become a spark. I guess I was both worried and kind of happy for him—if, you know, there was going to be a love story."

"Yeah . . . but I think they both got a lot of answers."

He nodded, his gaze perusing her. "Still planning on swimming?"

"As far as I know." Anita smiled. "I'm not really a swimsuit person, you know, since I'm not a runner like you."

Wyatt's brows raised. "What does that even mean?"

"It means that when we go to the pool, I read, and Carly swims," she said. "It also means that I've worn the same swimsuit for like ten years."

He smirked. "There's no swimsuit competition going on here." Then he paused. "That's not how I meant it."

"What did you mean?" she teased.

"I mean . . ." His gaze captured hers. "Whatever you wear, now or at a pool, you'll look beautiful."

She waved a hand. "You're just trying to butter me up to go on more road trips with you and your grandpa."

Wyatt laughed. "Yeah, that's totally it."

He was closer now, and Anita could practically feel the warmth radiating off his bare torso.

"For the record," he said in a quieter tone, "I just like being with you. Road trip or not. But I would like to take you to dinner after this trip. The two of us—if that would be okay with Carly?"

"I think it would be okay," she said, her stomach doing flips. "Would this dinner have a purpose?"

"Besides eating?" Wyatt asked. "It would."

Anita waited.

"It would be the first of many, I hope?" His mouth curved into a smile. "I like you, and I think you like me too.

And maybe . . ." His fingers grasped hers. "Maybe you'd let me kiss you?"

Her stomach did a full somersault. "That's a possibility." She inched closer. "But why wait?"

Wyatt's brows lifted, then his eyes grew intense. "You don't mind a hotel hallway?"

"I don't." It was the truth.

His smile grew, and his other hand slipped to her waist.

Anita wasn't sure what she was expecting or hoping for when Wyatt kissed her, but it wasn't supposed to be on her cheek.

"Hey," she protested.

He drew away, a grin on his face. "When I kiss you for real, it's not going to be when we could be interrupted at any moment."

She'd opened her mouth to reply, when the door opened behind her.

"All done," Carly said, her eyes bright as she looked from Anita to Wyatt. Their hands were still linked, so there was no hiding what was going on. "Ready to go swimming?"

"Ready," Wyatt said in a cheerful tone.

"We'll meet you there in a few minutes." Anita released his hand and headed into the room with her daughter.

Shutting the door, Carly spun and asked, "Were you guys kissing?"

"No," she said immediately. "We were talking about it, though."

Carly laughed. "Mom . . . you like him."

"I do," Anita replied, but she didn't really want this to be the topic of conversation when her head was buzzing with all that Wyatt had said. "What happened with the phone call with your dad? How did it go?"

Carly shrugged. "It was fine. He's not going to visit next

week, which I'm not surprised about. But we agreed to talk on the phone every week."

"Are you okay with that?"

"Yeah," she said. "I don't really know him, and I don't want to all of a sudden be dealing with awkward visits."

Anita blew out a breath. "Is there anything I can do?"

Carly raised her brows. "Get changed. I want to go swimming."

Anita smiled. Everything about this trip had been amazing, even with the harder things. Her relationship with Carly had matured and felt stronger than ever. She was handling her absent dad situation with grace. Sam and Susan had found closure. And Wyatt . . . he was quickly finding a place in her heart, and she didn't feel afraid about it.

Twenty minutes later, Carly and Wyatt were swimming against each other in some sort of very short lap race, and Anita sat on the edge of the hot tub.

She smiled when they finished, and somehow Carly was declared the winner even though from Anita's viewpoint, Wyatt had finished several feet ahead of her.

"I'm beat," he said, hoisting himself out of the pool. Dripping with water, he walked toward the hot tub.

Anita had trouble keeping her eyes off of his long frame and defined physique, but to be fair, Wyatt was looking at her too. "Nice swimsuit," he said.

"Is that a joke?" she asked.

He chuckled. "No. Like I told you, you look beautiful in anything."

Anita glanced down at her very basic black swimsuit with a sweetheart neckline. It was a bit frayed, but swimming wasn't really her thing, so why should she invest in it?

Wyatt slipped into the hot tub. "Are you coming in?"

She moved lower in the water until she was sitting on the protruding bench.

A young family arrived at the pool, and the two young kids immediately started talking to Carly and asking her questions.

"Looks like Carly has some fans," Wyatt said.

"She loves little kids." Anita moved her fingers along the surface of the bubbling water. "I've always felt a little bit guilty that she doesn't have any siblings. I mean, not that I wanted another baby with Bobby. But for Carly's sake, she would have been a great big sister."

"I get it," Wyatt said, his gaze moving to those in the pool. "Does she babysit other families?"

"Once in a while."

Somehow they'd migrated closer together, and their conversation felt almost private.

"I think a couple of kids would have been great, at least at one point," Wyatt said. "I'm probably too old now."

Anita scoffed. "Men don't age out like women do."

The edge of his mouth lifted. "True. Would you ever consider having more children, you know, if you found the right man?"

She knew her face had heated up, and not from the hot tub. "I don't think so. I mean, I'm thirty-five and would be considered high risk."

Wyatt didn't seem fazed at her reply, so she wasn't sure what all he meant.

"So . . . tell me about the woman who broke your heart."

He raised his arms and rested them on the edge of the hot tub. "Cynthia was a concert pianist. She also had an ex-husband she was still in love with. After we broke up, she went back to him, or maybe it was the other way around."

"Ouch," Anita said.

"Yeah, ouch." He held her gaze. "It was rough, but I think you've had it a bit rougher."

The Healing Garden

"Heartbreak can't be measured." She turned toward him more. "I'm sorry for what she put you through."

"I always thought I'd meet someone a lot earlier in my life and marry. You know, the traditional life."

Anita smiled. "Nothing's really traditional in life. At least not for everyone."

"True." Wyatt ran his fingers over her shoulder, and goose bumps dotted her skin.

In this moment, she wished they weren't surrounded by other people at a hotel pool. She wished it were just the two of them. On the other hand, she wouldn't trade these moments of Carly enjoying herself on a weekend trip and Sam finding closure on his past.

Twenty-four

"WHOSE CAR IS THAT?" CARLY pointed to Phyllis's house as Wyatt turned into their driveway.

They were finally home, and Sam had been dropped off. Both Anita and Carly had promised to visit him the next evening. It was strange how Anita missed him—as if he were her own grandpa.

"Oh, that must be Cameron's car." She squinted through the golden brightness of the setting sun. "I'll have to go over and ask how everything is going."

"Can I come?" Carly asked, nearly hopping out of the car before it was fully stopped.

"Of course," she said. "We need to take our stuff inside, though, and thank Wyatt."

"Oh right. Thanks Wyatt!" Carly grinned.

"You're welcome," he said. "And thanks to you and your mom for coming."

She shrugged and said to Anita, "After we talk to Cameron, can I call my friends?"

"Sure."

Carly shut the door and moved to the back of the car to wait for the trunk to open.

"She has way too much energy after being in a car all day," Anita commented.

Wyatt smirked. "Probably because she napped about as long Gramps."

The Healing Garden

"That's true. It might be a long night for both of us if she's not tired."

His expression sobered. "Thanks again, Anita. I know I've told you multiple times, but it was really good to have you and Carly along. Helped both me and Gramps."

Anita rested her hand on his arm. "I'm glad I got to meet Susan and her daughter."

Wyatt's gaze remained on hers, and she didn't want to look away. But Carly was waiting. Reluctantly she opened her door. He stepped out too. Opening the trunk, he carried their bags to the porch.

"Anything else?" he asked, smiling at Carly, then locking his gaze on Anita.

"No," she said breathlessly. "I—"

"Meow." Sassy appeared, leaping onto the porch from the front flowerbed where she must have been lounging.

"Sassy!" Carly scooped her up and buried her face in the cat's fur.

"Call when you have an update on your neighbor," Wyatt said softly, his gaze intent on Anita's.

His gaze said so much more, but there was too much going on for her to try to figure it out. "All right."

She watched Wyatt walk back to his car until Carly said, "Aren't you going to unlock the door?"

"Right." Anita fished out her keys from her purse, then opened the door. Once they had their bags inside and Carly had set down food for the cat, they headed over to Phyllis's place.

"It's weird to be here when she's gone," Carly mused after she rang the doorbell.

A woman answered the door. She looked to be around thirty, and she held a toddler on her hip. It had to be Cameron's wife, Becky.

"Hi," Anita said. "We live next door. Anita and Carly Gifford. We spoke with your husband earlier? Are you Becky?"

She flashed a dimpled smile. "Yes, that's right. Nice to meet you. Phyllis came home about an hour ago if you'd like to see her."

Anita's eyes widened. "She's home already?"

"The last twenty-four hours have been really good. She's doing so much better, so the doctor has assigned a physical therapist to come here three times a week. They think she'll make a full recovery."

"Oh wow," she breathed. "That's amazing."

Becky opened the door wider. "Come this way."

They followed her into the house, but instead of heading to the bedroom as she thought they might, Becky led them through the house to the backyard. There, on the back patio, Phyllis sat on a cushioned lounge chair, a throw blanket covering her legs. The yard and garden beyond her were bathed in soft orange light, a precursor to the approaching twilight.

"Well . . . my . . . favorite neighbors," Phyllis said in a cheery tone. Her hair had been brushed, but lacked its usual immaculately curled style. She didn't wear any lipstick or rouge, and the wrinkles in her skin seemed deeper. But it was still Phyllis. Dear Phyllis.

"How wonderful to see you up and about," Anita said.

Phyllis smiled and held out her hand.

Carly stepped forward and took it, then kissed her cheek. Anita did the same.

"I'll leave you three to visit," Becky said. "If you need anything, just holler." She walked back into the house.

"Becky said you're improving by leaps and bounds," Anita told Phyllis.

The Healing Garden

She sighed and adjusted her blanket. "I'm . . . fortunate. You . . . rescued me."

Anita and Carly sat on nearby chairs. "It was the middle of the night, and you had all your lights on," Carly said. "Mom broke into the house, then called nine-one-one and the ambulance came."

"I didn't exactly break in," she said with a laugh. "The door was unlocked."

"I . . . don't remember . . . leaving it unlocked." Phyllis rubbed at her temple. "Cameron and Becky . . . want to move in. I don't . . . know, though. I like my . . . own space."

Anita didn't know what to say. How much help would Phyllis need after her physical therapy appointments? She knew that stroke recovery couldn't be predicted. "It might be too early to make that big of a decision. Just be patient with yourself and your recovery."

"You're right," Phyllis said, then she turned to Carly. "Carly . . . your mother . . . is a smart woman."

Carly smiled. "I know. She always has good advice, but I don't think she's being smart about Wyatt."

"Wyatt?" Phyllis asked in an intrigued tone.

"Carly—" Anita started.

"He's the guy we met at the assisted living center," she said. "Don't worry, he's her age. It's his grandpa that we visit." She continued, laying out the entire story of Sam and Susan and their trip to Medford. She finished with, "They hold hands when they think I'm not looking, but I think they should start dating and kiss already."

"Carly!"

Phyllis laughed. "Wyatt . . . sounds wonderful . . . I agree with you, Carly . . . Anita needs to give . . . him a chance."

"I am giving him a chance," she said, sure her face was tomato red. "I have a lot of complications in my life, and I'm not looking for heartbreak."

"What kind of complications?" Carly folded her arms. "And Wyatt would never break your heart."

"Said the fourteen-year-old," Anita muttered under her breath.

"Mom, I've watched you date other men," Carly said. "Wyatt is different. From Glenn, from Dad, from anyone else. You don't have those frown lines on your forehead when you're around Wyatt."

Anita touched her forehead. "What are you talking about?"

"You get lines when you're dating someone," Carly continued. "But with Wyatt, they disappear."

"That's . . . observant," Phyllis said, a gleam in her eyes. "I'd like to meet him . . . officially."

Anita huffed out a breath. "We'll see. Now, Carly, we need to unpack and do laundry." She looked back to her neighbor. "Phyllis, I was wondering something. What if we created a connecting gate between our gardens? You know, so you can come over to my house without all the fuss of going around front?"

Phyllis's eyes gleamed. "I . . . would love that."

Anita squeezed her hand. "I would love it too. We could visit each other without all the formality."

Phyllis squeezed back.

"Can I visit again tomorrow? What's your schedule like?"

Phyllis grimaced. "Torturous physical therapy . . . in the morning. Come for lunch? Becky can fix us . . . sandwiches." She winked. "I have to put her . . . to work somehow."

"I'll bring dessert, then," Anita said with a laugh. "Then after school, Carly can pop in too."

"That would be lovely."

They left Phyllis, and after saying goodbye to Becky, headed back to the house.

The Healing Garden

"If you want to call Wyatt now, I can wait to call my friends," Carly offered.

Anita shook her head with a scoff. "You're so persistent—what's gotten into you?"

Her daughter just smiled and walked into their house.

"Go ahead and call your friends first."

Carly laughed as she headed down the hallway.

Anita opened the refrigerator, then the freezer. She decided to make a chicken casserole. She pulled out chicken and began to defrost it in a pan of hot water. They had peas and carrots and pasta . . . or should she make rice?

The doorbell rang, and for a moment, she wondered if it was Becky. Maybe they needed help with something, or to run an errand? As she neared the door, her heart skipped a beat at the thought of Wyatt showing up. But when she opened the door, her stomach knotted.

"Bobby?"

He smiled tentatively from his spot on the porch. In one hand, he held a small bouquet of flowers.

Anita could only stare at her ex-husband. Of course he knew where she lived, but he'd never come over like this. And Carly . . . He must be here to see Carly. Did she know? If so, why hadn't she said anything?

"Sorry for the surprise," Bobby said, his smile still in place, albeit nervous. "I seem to have a problem with follow-through. I thought if I just showed up, without making promises that I'd probably break, then I could see my daughter. You know, get those jitters out of the way."

Anita blinked. She had no idea what to say, or what to do . . .

"Mom?" Carly's voice came from behind her. She'd probably heard the doorbell too.

She closed her eyes, then felt Carly come to stand by her side.

"Hi, pumpkin," Bobby said.

Anita opened her eyes.

"Daddy?" Carly said in a quiet voice. Everything about her had gone still.

"These are for you," he said, holding up the flowers. "I know it's not much of an apology, but I was sorry to miss you last week."

Carly didn't move; Anita didn't move.

The seconds ticked by, and Bobby's smile faded. He lowered his arm. "If this isn't a good time, then maybe tomorrow? I'm back at my parents'. I, uh, things with Gloria went south. Again." He gave a nervous laugh. "Not that it should be a reason to see my daughter, or not see her." He blew out a breath and scrubbed his free hand through his hair. "Look. I'll call next time. But I just wanted to see you."

His gaze shifted to Carly again.

"Can he come in, Mom?" she said.

Anita opened her mouth to reply, but the words were stuck.

Carly seemed to recover much quicker than she. "Let's sit on the porch, Dad," she said. "We just got back from out of town, so I only have a few minutes."

Relief crossed Bobby's face, and Anita hated that she was glad to see it. Glad to see Carly's dad care about his daughter for a change.

"Great." He moved off the porch, and Carly sat down.

Anita left the door open as they sat down, a couple of feet between them.

She didn't want to eavesdrop, but she also didn't want Carly to feel like she was being cornered by her dad.

She walked to the kitchen and sat at the table. Emotions churned inside of her. This was good, right? Maybe Bobby had really turned a corner. Maybe he and Carly could have a positive relationship. She rose from the table and went about preparing the casserole. Maybe someday, she'd invite Bobby in. But it wouldn't be today.

When Carly came into the kitchen, she found a vase for the flowers.

"Did he leave?" Anita asked.

"Yeah. He'll be here all week, he said. And maybe on Friday, we'll have another visit."

"Are you all right?"

Carly nodded, but tears formed in her eyes.

Anita stepped close and pulled her into her arms. "I'm sorry it took him so long."

She sniffled. "Me too, but I'm not going to dwell on the past."

"Are you sure you're not twenty-five?"

Carly gave a muffled laugh, then drew away. "He asked about you . . . and I told him you have an amazing boyfriend."

"Uh, that's not true, and kind of dramatic."

Her daughter shrugged. "Well, it can be true."

She only sighed. "All right. You win. I'll call Wyatt after dinner."

"Good." Carly moved past her. "I need to get started on my homework. Call me when dinner's ready."

Anita stared after her. She sensed Carly wanted some time to herself, but her daughter was growing up before her eyes. Becoming a responsible adult. Anita knew she had Sam to thank for a portion of that. As well as Wyatt. And Phyllis. How did she get so lucky to have such amazing role models for Carly just when she needed them?

It ended up being nearly ten p.m. when Anita finally called Wyatt. She wondered if it might be late for him, since he ran early in the morning. But he answered almost immediately.

"Hey, it's Anita."

"Hey. I'm glad you called."

This alerted her. "Is everything all right with your grandpa?"

"Oh sure," he said in a soft voice. "I just didn't know if you'd gotten sick of me on our trip. We were together a lot."

A laugh burst out. "No, I didn't get sick of you, and neither did Carly. She kept reminding me to call you. She told Phyllis that you're my boyfriend."

"Is that right?" Wyatt paused. "How is Phyllis?"

Anita gave him the update, then he asked, "Are you calling because you want to or because of Carly?"

She didn't have to think about that. "It's all me, Wyatt."

"That's good to hear," he said slowly. "Are we going on a date, then? Because if I'm going to be your boyfriend, I think it's a good idea."

Heat filled her chest. "Are you asking?"

"Always."

Anita's smile felt like a permanent fixture on her face. "I'm free on Thursday night."

"It's a deal."

"Although..."

"Although what?" he asked.

"That does seem far away, even though we'll see you at the center tomorrow night."

"Thursday *is* really far away," Wyatt said, "when I kind of want to see you tonight."

Anita's breath stalled. "It's after ten o'clock."

"I'm not tired," he said in a teasing tone.

But she didn't want him to be teasing. "I'm not either."

"Did you just invite me over?"

"Yes." She wasn't going to beat around the bush. She did want to see him again, and the sooner the better. "But I should warn you. Bobby came over tonight—surprised us both—and it was a lot to take in. Carly was a trooper, though."

"Oh wow, that's . . . good I guess? In the long run?"

"I'm hoping so." Anita released a breath. "Carly is a smart girl and a realist."

"She gets that from her mom."

"Hmm."

"Do you still want me to come over?" Wyatt asked. "Or do you need some time to yourself?"

"I need some time with you," she said immediately.

"Then see you soon," he rumbled.

After they hung up, Anita hurried to her bedroom and changed back into regular clothing. She couldn't see him in her ratty sweats. She had a feeling he wouldn't mind much, but she wasn't ready to advance their relationship to that stage.

By the time she saw the red Cadillac's headlights swing into her driveway, she was sitting on the front porch with the light off to keep the neighbors from spying too much.

He climbed out and seemed to spot her immediately as he walked toward the porch. He wore a fitted T-shirt and those jeans of his she liked, his smile just for her.

"Hey," she said.

"Hey. Good to see you again."

She laughed, then stepped into his arms and hugged him. She was done holding back with this man. He pulled her close, and she shut her eyes to breathe in his clean scent. "Thanks for coming," she whispered.

"Anytime."

She drew away and looked up at him. His gaze was intent on hers. Now was the time. She was done waiting.

"Come into the backyard."

She slipped her hand into his, then tugged him with her. They walked around the house, moonlight bathing the ground. "I told Phyllis we should make a connecting gate between our backyards."

"I can help."

Anita smiled up at him. "You're volunteering. Just like that?"

"I am."

"Well, you're hired, then."

They slowed their steps by one of the flowering bushes. They were isolated from the street and from any neighbors' windows. It was just the two of them, at last.

"Kiss me, Wyatt."

"I was hoping you'd ask," he whispered, his hands finding her hips and drawing her close.

Her heart felt like it was going to pound out of her chest as his lips brushed against hers, warm and soft. Tentative. But she didn't want a tentative kiss.

She moved her hands behind his neck and tugged him closer as a breeze picked up, bringing with it the scent of the garden.

He smiled against her mouth, and then he was kissing her like he meant it. Everywhere he touched her, little flames ignited. She couldn't remember feeling this mixture of comfort and desire ever with another man. Her relationship with Bobby had been full of too many insecurities. With Wyatt, deep down, she knew she could trust him. She knew he was real, and that his heart was good.

She let herself fall into him, to receive what he was giving, and to focus on him, and only him. His smile, his touch, his mouth on hers, and her heart was soaring, her stomach spinning, and her feet floating.

"Anita," he said, drawing away slightly. "Is that Sassy?"

She took a second to catch her breath, then looked down. Sassy was weaving between Wyatt's ankles.

"Hey, Sassy, can you give us some privacy?"

Wyatt chuckled and moved his thumb along her jaw, then over her bottom lip. The intensity of his gaze told her what he wasn't saying in words. He closed the distance to kiss her again, his mouth exploring, and her skin heating again. Her entire body was humming, and she knew she'd never forget this first kiss from Wyatt, even though she planned on enjoying a lot more.

Sassy, of course, completely ignored Anita's request, but if Wyatt didn't mind, then she could ignore the cat.

"Is this where I ask you to be my girlfriend?" he murmured.

She moved her fingers over his shoulders and rested her hands on his biceps. She could see the glint of his eyes in the moonlight. "I think it's perfect timing."

His smile was slow, warming her to her toes. "Will you be my girlfriend, Anita?"

"I will, Wyatt."

He drew her close and hugged her tightly.

"Meow."

Anita laughed. "I think I'd better let her in the house, or she'll not leave us alone." She released him. "Do you want to stay for a bit?"

He grasped her hand and linked their fingers. "I'm not going anywhere."

Epilogue

Six months later

"So this is the place?" Susan asked, settling into a chair with the help of Lila.

Anita smiled at the visitors to the assisted living center. It was currently decked out with holiday decorations, a mixture of Christmas and Hannukah. She and Wyatt sat together at the table, holding hands, waiting for Carly to return with a couple of board games. The room was filled with visiting families, and conversation and laughter buzzed around them.

Sam beamed down at Susan, one hand gripping his walker. "This is the place. There's an opening if you want to join me."

Anita's heart almost melted.

Susan's blue eyes sparkled. "Don't tempt me."

With careful movements, Sam transitioned from the walker and sat in the chair next to Susan. "That's exactly what I'm hoping to do. Tempt you."

"Oh, Sam." She patted his arm, then shook her head. "Let's take this a day at a time."

Wyatt nudged Anita, and she smiled. It was definitely amusing to watch the elderly couple across from them flirt.

"What did I miss?" Paula asked, arriving at the table with a festive green bag slung over her shoulder.

The Healing Garden

Sam looked up as she bent to kiss his cheek. "I'm trying to convince Susan to come to the center," he said with a wave of his hand. "She's being stubborn as usual."

"I'm sure you'll charm her into it eventually," Paula said with a wink. "Now, I've brought gifts for everyone." She set the green bag onto the table with a thump.

"For me too?" Carly asked, appearing just then with a stack of board games in her arms.

"Yes, my almost-niece."

Anita's gaze snapped to Paula. *What* had she said?

Paula's face pinked, and she covered her mouth with one hand. "Oh no. I'm *so* sorry." She closed her eyes, dragged in a breath, then opened her eyes again. "Forget I said anything. Rewind. Delete. Erase."

Wyatt was still holding Anita's hand, but he'd grown very still. Not moving, not looking at her, not saying anything.

Her mind raced. She didn't know what to think. What to infer. Maybe it was nothing. Maybe . . .

"Presents, anyone?" Paula said in a too-bright tone. She began to pull out gift-wrapped boxes from the bag. "This one is for . . . Gramps." She handed over a red box with a gold bow. "And . . . Susan."

"You didn't have to do this, dear," she said, but accepted the gift with a smile.

The next gift Paula pulled out was a rectangular box. "Carly—here's yours."

"Oh thanks," she quipped. "Can I open it tonight?"

"Of course," Paula said. "Waiting until Christmas is lame."

Carly laughed.

Paula busied herself pulling out another present. "Lila, this is for you."

"Thank you so much," she said, a flush to her cheeks. "I wasn't expecting a gift exchange. Sorry I didn't—"

Paula waved a hand. "You're fine. Christmas is kind of my thing, and I'm not expecting any gifts in return. I'm just excited for the holidays, and we're all grateful that you brought Susan to visit.

"And next," she continued, taking out two smaller boxes. "For you, brother, and your sweetheart." Her brows waggled as she handed over Wyatt's gift.

Anita accepted the box from her. It was the same size as Wyatt's.

"All right, everyone." Paula waved her hands. "Open your gifts. The suspense is killing me."

"At the same time?" Carly asked.

"Yes," she said with a laugh.

The paper tearing commenced.

Anita loved how spontaneous Paula was, and she loved how Wyatt was the opposite—methodical and scheduled and organized. She loved *him*. Absolutely and completely. She'd confessed her feelings last month, and he'd told her he loved her as well, and it had felt like the most natural thing in the world. After all, they spent almost every day together, including weekends. Either visiting Gramps, taking Carly to a movie or another outing, or sometimes just hanging out at home—preparing dinner together, then watching the sunset from the garden bench.

Wyatt had done ninety-nine percent of the work on building a connecting gate to Phyllis's backyard, and he even helped Cameron renovate a few things in Phyllis's house so things would be more accessible as she continued to recover. Cameron and Becky had sold their condo and moved in permanently with Phyllis, bringing plenty of life to the house and neighborhood with their toddler.

The Healing Garden

Wyatt had finally met Bobby, and it seemed that Bobby was committed to becoming a permanent part of Carly's life. They saw each other nearly every week, and Carly seemed to enjoy her daddy-daughter dates. She had a sweet relationship with Wyatt as well. They could joke around, but she'd also listen to his advice about more serious things. All in all, gratitude brimmed in Anita's heart for everyone at this table.

"Wow, I love it, Paula," Carly declared, holding up a Rubik's Cube. "My friend Sara is a whiz at these, but now I can practice at home on my own."

"Happy to hear it," she said. "Merry Christmas."

As the others were exclaiming over their gifts and thanking Paula, Anita opened her box to find a gold bracelet interlinked with painted ceramic butterflies. "It's beautiful. Thank you, Paula."

Paula grinned, then looked at Wyatt and mouthed, "I'm sorry."

He gave a small shake of his head, and she mimed zipping her lips.

"What's going on with you and Paula?" Anita asked him in a quiet voice. He didn't have to tell her, but she was too curious not to ask.

"It's..." he began.

"It's nothing," Paula said with a wave of her hand. "I mean, it's something, but not what you're thinking or what I implied."

Apparently, everyone had paused in their gift opening to watch and listen.

"Continue," Paula said. "Ignore everything I say tonight. I'm the worst at keeping secrets." She shook her head and began to collect the discarded wrappings. "There I go again! Now, who wants to play Scrabble?"

No one answered. Everyone stared at Paula.

"Say something, Wyatt." She turned her pleading gaze to her brother. "Bail me out here."

His mouth edged into a smile. Then he looked at Anita. "I was planning on doing this a little later tonight, but I guess there's no reason to wait. If I do, then Paula will just keep putting her foot in her mouth."

"What are you talking about?" Anita asked.

He shifted away from her, moved off his chair, and knelt close to her.

Why was he kneeling. *Oh* . . . She drew in a sharp breath. "Wyatt . . ." she whispered.

Not only had those at the table gone silent, but the entire room had hushed. Did everyone know what was going on but her?

"Anita, you know I love you," he said quietly, but somehow it seemed to fill the room. "And I'll keep telling you every day because I love you more than anything else in the world."

His green eyes were so intense and so full of love that Anita felt tears burn.

"I'd be honored if you'd marry me and become my wife," he said in that low voice she loved. He took the small box he'd unwrapped earlier, and only now did Anita realize he hadn't actually opened it. Now, he did.

Inside was a gold ring, inset with a diamond and two rubies. "This was my grandmother's, and I want the love of my life to wear it."

Anita's tears spilled over, and she looked from the ring to Wyatt. His expression was full of that love and devotion she'd come to cherish, come to rely on. "It's beautiful, Wyatt," she whispered. "Are you sure about this ring?"

"He has my permission," Sam said from across the table, his voice cracking. "The ring is meant to be worn, and I can't think of anyone else I'd rather wear Norma's ring. I've never seen my grandson so happy."

She brushed at the tears on her cheeks.

"If I wasn't clear before, will you marry me, Anita?" Wyatt asked in a teasing tone.

"Say yes, Mom," Carly said.

Anita smiled and drew in a shaky breath. "Yes, Wyatt, I'll marry you."

He grinned, and she threw her arms about his neck. Cheers erupted around them, but Anita could only think of the man in her arms, the man who held her heart, the man who'd given her a second life.

Wyatt pulled her close and murmured in her ear, "I love you."

"I love you, too," she said, holding on to him for a long moment.

When they drew apart, Carly was there to hug her.

"I'm proud of you, Mom," she said, and Anita laughed. "Now try on the ring. I want to see what it looks like."

Anita wiped away more tears, then she let Wyatt slip on the ring. Turning her hand, she watched the diamond and rubies catch the light.

"Beautiful," he said, his arm coming around her as he kissed her temple.

She looked over at her new family-to-be. Paula was beaming, Sam had his hand over Susan's, and Susan had tears in her eyes.

"I can't wait to call my friends and tell them," Carly said. Then her eyes widened. "Can I be a bridesmaid?"

"Of course," Anita said with a laugh. Marriage. A wedding. Her mind was spinning.

She turned toward Wyatt and wrapped her arms about his waist. He leaned down and kissed her, lingering until Paula nudged them.

"Hey, I want to hug my new sister-in-law too."

Wyatt released Anita, and she hugged Paula. "How long have you known?"

Paula drew away. "Oh, I've known for months, possibly since that first night I met you. It only took my brother a little longer to realize that you were his future."

"Not that much longer," Wyatt said, his gaze finding Anita's.

She lifted her face to his, and he kissed her again.

"All right, all right," Paula said, lifting her hands. "I'll get out of the way."

"Are you two going to keep smooching, or are you playing Scrabble?" Sam asked.

Wyatt released Anita with a grin. "It's up to my fiancée."

She smirked. "I'll just watch. I think my brain is too scrambled to spell out any words."

Sitting at the table, Anita linked her fingers with Wyatt's and leaned her head on his shoulder. She watched the game unfold. Carly's triumph. Sam's competitive spirit. Susan smiling at everything he said. Paula coming up with the wackiest words possible. Lila helping her mother sort through word combinations.

And Wyatt . . . the way he kept her hand, his fingers strong and sure and warm. Locking in their future together. And Anita knew there was nowhere else she wanted to be.

Continue reading for a Sneak Peek of the
next book in the series, THE HEALING SUMMER:

One

Seattle
Summer, 1981

JO SAMPSON KNEW LIFE COULD always be worse. Logic—plus an MFA and doctorate in history—told her that life was often worse. Yet, today made her top five list of worst days.

"Mo-om." Alec's thirteen-year-old voice cracked as he called to her from the bottom of the stairs.

Jo had brought the large white envelope upstairs to her bedroom to open in privacy. But she'd forgotten to shut the door, so her solitude had ended before she could finish reading through the copy her lawyer had sent of her final, signed divorce papers.

"The taxi's going to leave," Alec hollered. "I'm getting in with or without you. I'll call you from a pay phone when I get to the airport."

If it had been any other day, when Jo's divorce papers weren't a glaring white rectangle on the new violet bedspread she'd bought after Liam moved out, she might have laughed at her son's declaration.

"I'm coming." Jo hoped the tremble didn't sound in her

voice. "I'm coming," she whispered to herself as she slipped the papers into the envelope. She already knew what they said, and what did it matter, anyway?

Her fourteen-year marriage was officially over.

Today, she'd drop her son at the airport to spend the summer with his dad and Liam's new fiancée in their new home in San Diego, where Alec would meet his new puppy...

New. New. New.

Jo didn't like all this *new*.

And she didn't really like her son flying so far on his own, but Alec had said he'd be fine. Liam said he'd be fine. So Jo had to live with it.

A soft snore came from the end of the bed. Speaking of old versus new. Jo had been left with the old dog—Sadie—and the old house. One hundred years old, to be exact. The house, not the dog.

When she'd first awakened this morning, hovering in the gray area between sleep and wakefulness, for several blessed seconds, she hadn't remembered all the changes in her life. Then the ache in her heart began before her brain even comprehended the changes of the past four months and three days.

Jo blinked away the burning in her eyes as she heard the front door open, and Alec holler another threat as his suitcase made that clickety-clack sound across the porch.

"Happy birthday to me," Jo whispered.

Sadie lifted her head for a moment, her sleepy eyes seeming to say, "Sorry you're not having a good birthday." But then her eyes slipped closed, and the snores started again. Sadie was ten, but she acted like she was fifty.

Releasing a sigh, Jo turned from the white envelope on the bed, and the sleeping dog, and left her bedroom. As she descended the stairs, she tried not to think of the hours and hours she and Liam had spent upgrading this one-hundred-year-old house. She loved everything about it, from the new banister, to the refinished hardwood floor, to the paint colors of Arctic Cotton and Misty Surf she'd chosen, to the chandelier she'd found at a swap meet hanging in the front entrance.

Jo grabbed her purse from the hall table, refinished only last summer when she was living a different life—a life she had no part of now. She walked through the open front door, and indeed, Alec was making good on his promise.

He had the trunk of the taxi open and was lifting his suitcase into it. His face had reddened, and his muscles strained. What in the world had he packed?

"Let me help you," Jo called to him. She locked the front door, then hurried to help her son.

Surprisingly, he waited for her, instead of proceeding with his usual stubbornness to do everything himself.

Jo grasped one side of the suitcase and lifted, then groaned. "What did you put in this?"

Alec pushed up the black-framed glasses on his nose. The gesture was so like Liam that a pang shot through Jo. Alec also resembled Liam, with his sandy-brown hair and studious green eyes. Jo had first noticed Liam's eyes when she met him in a faculty meeting at Seattle Central College.

"I want to show Dad my geode collection," Alec said in that no-nonsense tone he'd perfected.

Of course, he does. Liam was a science teacher, and Alec's interests were heading in that direction, too. "You know the weight limit is fifty pounds on the plane?"

"You can bring something heavier," Alec informed her. "They put on a tag and charge extra. Mrs. Howard told me."

Leave it to Alec to ask for advice from their world-traveling neighbor, Maggie Howard. Jo decided she was too tired to argue with her son about the wisdom of hauling rocks on a plane ride. "All right, lift on three."

Once the suitcase was inside the trunk of the car, Jo said, "Don't you want to say goodbye to Sadie?"

"I already did," Alec said. "When you were in the shower."

At least there was that. Alec was still loyal to his dog—a dog that Jo remembered finding with Liam. Another memory she'd have to stuff away. She rerouted herself back to the present and greeted the taxi driver, an older woman who had more colors in her hair than Jo could identify.

"There's Mrs. Howard," Alec said as they pulled onto the street.

Jo looked over to see their elderly neighbor out walking in her slow gait. Maggie Howard was a quiet woman, but she faithfully walked the neighborhood each day. The sight always inspired Jo to exercise herself—another goal she was determined to achieve this summer.

Jo and Alec waved as they passed the woman and Mrs. Howard waved back, her eyes as sharp as ever. The few times Jo had visited Maggie's home, she had been impressed with the woman's collection of art. Everything from seascapes to miniature portraits from sixteenth-century Europe decorated the woman's walls.

Maggie's husband had been an innovator of dental implants, and he'd traveled the world presenting at medical conferences. Maggie went along and collected art. A charmed life, if there ever was one, Jo decided.

The taxi continued out of the neighborhood, and the driver kept up a friendly and steady chatter with Alec as they drove to the Seattle airport.

Jo felt grateful for the driver's distraction because the reality of Alec's leaving was starting to settle in. She'd already determined not to cry at the airport—after Alec had made her promise, of course. Besides, having her son away for the summer would theoretically allow Jo plenty of time to work on that historical study about Mongol queens she'd started three years ago. The research had been fascinating, but with everyone home during the summers—Liam was on the same professor schedule—writing had always taken a back seat.

No more delays, Jo determined, trying not to feel the impact of the reason *why* she'd now finally have so much uninterrupted time. Alec would be gone, and her marriage was over.

"Which terminal?" the taxi driver asked.

Before Jo could answer, Alec did it for her.

As the driver pulled to the curb, the impact that Alec would really be leaving, and the time was now, made Jo's eyes sting.

"You're not going to cry, are you, Mom?" Alec said from the back seat.

Jo dragged in a breath. "Of course, not," she said in a cheerful, albeit wobbly, tone. She was probably not even fooling the taxi driver. She popped open her door and told the driver, "Maybe you'll be my return trip home."

As it turned out, Jo reemerged from the airport an hour-and-a-half later, when she knew Alec's plane had left the ground. After her tears had dried, she'd called Liam from a pay phone to let him know that the flight was on time, and only when he confirmed he'd be there to pick up Alec did she leave the terminal to find another taxi.

Jo would have driven, but her car was in the shop. Her second taxi driver of the day was a young man, twentysomething, who talked about his hobby of painting miniature board game creatures. Jo had never heard of such a thing and wanted to ask Liam about it. But then she remembered. She couldn't ask Liam. Well, it would be very awkward if she did. It wasn't like they were enemies, but they weren't really friends, either. Not anymore.

"It's not you, it's me," Liam had told her on that rainy day in early February. "Things have been off between us for a while. I don't feel myself anymore, and you don't deserve half a husband."

Jo had wanted to ask him what he meant by "a while," but she was too numb to ask those types of questions. He moved out the week before Valentine's Day, and on Valentine's night, while Jo was on her second bowl of ice cream, Alec had called her from Liam's apartment, where he was spending the weekend, and asked her why Dad had taken another woman to dinner.

On Liam's parenting weekend, he'd gone on a date and left Alec home alone. Jo had then known the truth about Liam's leaving her.

When the taxi turned onto her street, Jo realized she'd tuned out whatever the driver had been speaking about in the last ten minutes. When he pulled into her driveway, she thanked him and paid, then climbed out.

Now, her summer was about to begin, and as she walked up the steps to her front door, she decided that today, she could review her manuscript pages. Then tomorrow, she'd go to the library to do research after she got her car out of the shop.

Since today was her birthday, she'd order pizza for dinner. Weren't fortieth birthdays supposed to be a bigger deal than normal? She'd order the kind of pizza *she* liked, and not the kind she always ordered for Liam and Alec to make them happy. It wasn't like she had a group of girlfriends to go out with. Any co-workers had been Liam's friends to begin with. Jo had just been the wife. Besides, it was hard to pin down any of their colleagues in the summer.

The Healing Garden

Jo and Liam. Liam and Jo. They always got smiles about the combination of their names. Now, it was just *Jo.* And *Liam and Krista.*

Jo told herself she would be happy with the homemade card and hand-me-down Rubik's Cube from Alec. It was sweet of him to give it to her. He had two others, but he'd said that his first was his favorite. And she couldn't really expect a thirteen-year-old kid to go out and get her a gift on his own. That would have been what Liam and Alec did together.

When she unlocked the front door and stepped into the house, the empty quiet was like a blow to her stomach. She shut the door with a quiet click, then stood in the entryway and listened to the clock hanging above the bottom stairs ticking. She couldn't remember the last time the house had been quiet enough to hear the ticking of a clock.

The memory of when she had bought the clock flashed through her mind. She and Liam had been at an antique store in downtown Seattle, and they'd browsed the store together, walking hand in hand. Jo had pulled Liam to a stop when she saw the clock—the Roman numerals against the mosaic background had practically yelled at her to take notice.

"Buy it," Liam had said, squeezing her hand.

"I don't dare look at the price," Jo told him.

She held her breath as Liam reached for the hanging white tag and turned it over. "Three-hundred and fifty."

Jo sighed. "Too much."

Liam released her hand, grasped the clock with both hands, and took it down from its spot on the wall. "Happy anniversary, sweetheart." He leaned close and kissed her.

Now, Jo closed her eyes. How long ago had that been? Five years? *Six?* She leaned against the front door, not wanting to walk farther into the house. Every item and every room would bring back another memory. Jo imagined herself by the end of the night lying on the floor, beneath the weight of too many memories. All of them had been tainted now.

Liam had fallen in love with another woman, and here Jo stood alone in the entryway of her beautiful home. Feeling as empty as the house.

When a knock sounded at the door, Jo startled.

Heart pounding, she swallowed back her surprise, then checked the peephole. Seconds later, Jo pulled the door open, a forced smile on her face, as she greeted her neighbor, Maggie Howard.

Two

MAGGIE DECIDED THAT JO SAMPSON looked as if she'd seen a ghost.

"I'm not dead yet," Maggie said.

Jo blinked, and her smile faltered. Yet her voice was perfectly sweet when she replied, "Hello, Maggie. What brings you here today?"

Maggie wasn't fooled for a moment. This woman had been crying, and by the looks of it, she needed a square meal. Or three. Her long, brunette hair was pulled into a high ponytail, and her normally warm brown eyes looked dull. "I've come to give you a birthday present."

The brown face of a dog nudged between Jo and the doorframe. "Hello, Sadie," Maggie said promptly. This family had the most mellow dog in the county, and Maggie wondered if the creature ever barked.

Jo patted Sadie's head, then met Maggie's gaze. "I . . . How did you know it was my birthday?" Jo raised her dark brows. She was one of those women who wore her emotions on her face.

Maggie had learned a long time ago to hide her regrets and painful memories. It was better that way. She couldn't bear the look of pity in another person's eyes when they learned all that Maggie had suffered.

Goodness, the woman looked as if she were about to

cry. "Never mind that." Maggie didn't want to admit that she remembered dates and events all too well. The good along with the bad. "You're forty? A girl's fortieth birthday can't go by without a celebration, right?"

"Right," Jo said in a faint voice.

Sadie plopped down at Jo's feet, a bored expression on her face.

Maggie refocused on Jo. The woman really needed a few days in the sun—maybe at the beach, although the Washington shoreline wasn't the warmer Californian beach. Maggie pushed any thoughts of California from her mind—for now. There would be plenty of time later, when she was alone, to indulge in those old memories.

"I'm taking you to dinner," Maggie continued. "And you're driving."

The smile that spread on Jo's face was genuine. At last. "I'm driving, huh?" Then her smile dimmed. "Except my car's in the shop. I had to take Alec to the airport in a taxi earlier."

Maggie nodded. She'd seen the taxi, and that forlorn look on Jo's face. It was what had prompted her to put this plan together. "We can take Herb," she said. "He hasn't been out in a while."

"You still have your Lincoln?"

"That I do," Maggie said. "Although they took away my license, it doesn't mean I had to give up my car, too."

"Okay," Jo said, her tone sounding brighter.

Maggie had done the right thing after all. "Are you available in about an hour? Herb doesn't like to deal with traffic."

Jo smiled at that.

"And once it gets dark," Maggie continued, "I like to be home sipping my orange tea."

The Healing Garden

Jo looked as if she might say no, but then she said, "All right. Do you have a place in mind?"

"Well, it's *your* birthday, but I do love Italian," Maggie said. "Have you tried Bello's?"

"I haven't, is it new?" Jo asked.

"No, it's been there since the sixties." Maggie really shouldn't torture herself by going there again, but she was like a moth flying straight toward a flame.

Jo nodded. "How fancy is this place?"

"Fancy," Maggie said. "Dress up."

Moments later, when Maggie was making her slow way back to her neighboring home, she found that she was smiling to herself. Nights out were rare for her, and at age ninety-four, she didn't dare drive herself. That, and the fact she'd lost her license three years ago. Couldn't pass the driving test. The Parkinson's medication she took compromised her reaction time should someone suddenly brake in front of her.

Maggie stopped when another neighbor's cat streaked across her path. "What are you up to, Sergeant?" she called after the gray tabby. The cat didn't respond but continued to the other side of the road. She and Bruce had never had pets on account of Bruce's allergies. Maybe she should get a cat or a dog now.

She turned up the walk to her stately two-story home. She'd lived here most of her married life, and she still remembered the day she and her husband bought it.

"I'd give you the world if I could, Maggie," Bruce had said. "But this house will have to do."

Maggie had laughed and hugged him. The house represented all her dreams for the future, hoping the five bedrooms would soon be filled with children, laughter, and love. But the children had never come. Only miscarriages.

After the seventh miscarriage, Bruce had sat her down on their pristine couch. Told her he wanted his wife back, that he loved her whether or not they had children, and he was going to take her to his next convention in Europe.

When Maggie had packed for the trip, she felt as if she were packing away her dreams of having children. Buckling up her suitcase had brought finality to her hope of becoming a mother. By the time she stepped off the plane in Paris, she'd reconciled herself to her new life. She hadn't expected to be so charmed by the museums of Europe. While Bruce met with medical experts, Maggie had visited museums, libraries, antique shops, and gift boutiques.

Her first art purchase was a painting of the French seashore at dawn. The artist had captured the pinks and golds of the early dawn light as it reflected off the sea. She'd never heard of the painter, but the shop owner said that he was well-known throughout Europe.

Maggie opened the door to her house and made a beeline for the kitchen. The walk to Jo's had winded her for some reason, and she needed some restorative tea. Or perhaps she was feeling faint because of the anticipation of asking Jo something important over dinner. If Jo turned her down, then Maggie didn't know what she would do.

She set a teakettle of water on the stove, then waited for the water to boil. Maggie didn't mind living alone for the most part. Bruce had been gone for years, and her only regret was her oldest regret—no children, no little Bruces or Maggies. And as a result, no grandchildren. Bruce had amassed a sizable fortune, and upon his death, Maggie had found she had no personal use for it. She continued to donate to her favorite charities and even bought a few more paintings. But shopping from catalogs was not the same thing as wandering through antique shops in Budapest or Liverpool.

The Healing Garden

The teakettle hissed, and Maggie removed it, then poured the hot water into a porcelain mug. Next, she added a tea bag of her favorite variety. She enjoyed the sweet flavor of the orange, and she always added cinnamon and honey to make it more robust.

Maggie took her time sipping her tea before reaching for the scrapbook she'd been adding to over the years. She'd shown it to Bruce once early in their marriage when it had only been about twenty pages long, and she found that answering his questions about her young life had only brought her more heartache.

If she kept her memories to herself, she could hold them close, and live a life beyond the pain.

If she shared her past, the pain grew and grew until she felt as if she were drowning.

But every year on the anniversary of her last day in San Francisco, she allowed herself an afternoon of going through the scrapbook. She hadn't added to it since Bruce's death. She wasn't sure why. Perhaps it was because she felt if she were to put anything into a scrapbook, it should include things about Bruce and their life together.

Since today was the anniversary of the day she'd left San Francisco for good, she'd indulge in looking at the pages again. She wondered how many more times she'd do this. Ninety-four years of age was nothing to sniff over, and she had no idea how much longer she'd live. Months? Years? More and more people were living into their nineties, yet Maggie couldn't expect that *he* was still alive. If he were, he'd be the remarkable age of ninety-six, for he'd been two years older than Maggie's nineteen when she'd met him that fateful day of April 18, 1906.

Orlando Gallo.

Just thinking his name sent a warm shiver along

Maggie's arms. Could he still be alive? Did he still remember her? Surely, he had dozens of grandchildren and possibly great-grandchildren. Italians always had large families; it was almost a religion.

Maggie wondered whom Orlando had married. Was she Italian? Did they stay in San Francisco? Did he ever become a famous artist? At least in his own right?

Maggie could admit that her interest in art had begun with Orlando. She could also admit that she'd been disappointed time and time again when she'd written to art galleries, first in San Francisco, then throughout the state and other surrounding states, inquiring if they'd ever heard of an artist by the name of Orlando Gallo.

Every response she'd received had been in the negative.

So, she was left to wonder all these years.

When she'd met with her estate manager last week, an idea had formed. What if she tracked down Orlando's descendants and left her estate to them? They could divide up the money from the trust fund and the sale of the home. It would be her way to thank Orlando for saving her life. But then the doubts set in. She was ninety-four. She couldn't very well drive herself down the Pacific coast. How would she find a man from seventy years ago? He could be dead. He could have moved across the country. Maybe he'd never married at all.

But the idea had kept Maggie awake at night. She had to try, and tonight, she'd present her plan to Jo. And God willing, Jo would agree to help Maggie find Orlando.

Find *THE HEALING SUMMER* at a retailer near you!

Heather B. Moore is a *USA Today* bestselling author of more than ninety publications. Heather writes primarily historical and #herstory fiction about the humanity and heroism of the everyday person. Publishing in a breadth of genres, Heather dives into the hearts and souls of her characters, meshing her love of research with her love of storytelling.

Her historicals and thrillers are written under pen name H.B. Moore. She writes women's fiction, romance, and inspirational non-fiction under Heather B. Moore, and . . . speculative fiction under Jane Redd. This can all be confusing, so her kids just call her Mom. Heather attended Cairo American College in Egypt and the Anglican School of Jerusalem in Israel. Despite failing her high school AP English exam, Heather persevered and earned a Bachelor of Science degree from Brigham Young University in something other than English.

For book updates, sign up for Heather's email list:
hbmoore.com/contact
Website: HBMoore.com
Instagram: @authorhbmoore
Facebook: Fans of Heather B. Moore

Blog: MyWritersLair.blogspot.com
Pinterest: HeatherBMoore
TikTok: https://www.tiktok.com/@heatherbmooreauthor
X: @HeatherBMoore

www.ingramcontent.com/pod-product-compliance
Lightning Source LLC
LaVergne TN
LVHW010157070526
838199LV00062B/4391